The Time of Our Life:
Decisions

Ian Sutton

i

Table of Contents

Introduction

"We have no sense of what's coming. Like a lot of big questions, it's going to take a crisis or a catastrophe before people start paying attention." – Planning Professor Carlton Basmajian, Iowa State University

"No one has any idea what the world will look like in 20 years." – Historian and philosopher Yuval Noah Harari (2024)

Each of us has a responsibility to our loved ones, as well as to ourselves, to manage the final departure of family members in the most respectful way possible.

As responsible members of the human race, we have an obligation to existing and future generations, amid numerous threats, to make those decisions and pay equal respect to the world we inhabit.

Flame cremation, which started becoming popular in the mid-20th century, was considered by many to be better for the environment than traditional burial that involves embalming, heavy caskets, and expensive cemetery space. However, it actually poses a serious threat to the environment. Fortunately, new options are emerging that allow families to make decisions that are respectful to their loved ones and to the planet.

How will society manage the deaths of billions over the remaining decades of this century and beyond? We must do all in our power to protect the kind of global environment we leave by choosing methods that minimize the impact on the planet.

The United Nations has forecast annual global deaths to reach almost 68 million in the year 2030, 80 million in 2040, 92 million in 2050, and 122.9 million in 2100, offset by 110 million births. That makes a cumulative total of more than 7.5 billion deaths from all causes between now and the end of the century. (United Nations, World Population Prospects)

The World Health Organization has called the 2000s 'the century of the elderly.' By 2040, people over 65 will make up almost a quarter of the U.S. population.

In 2030, when the global population is projected to reach more than 8 billion, 1.4 billion of us will be over 60, and there will be 9 million of the 'oldest of the old,' those born prior to and during World War II. The population is expected to grow to 9.8 billion by 2050, and those over 60 to more than 2 billion.

Some projections forecast the population will reach 11.2 billion by the end of the century, but another recent UN report suggests a falling birthrate will stall population growth starting by 2050. World population will peak at about 10.3 billion in the mid-2080s before starting to decline as deaths begin to outnumber births in many countries. By 2100, there may be as few as 6 billion people on Earth, this study predicts.

The shift in global demographics will have significant societal, economic, and geopolitical implications for countries around the world, requiring governments to plan for aging populations, potential workforce shortages, and other challenges.

The United Nations, at the same time, forecasts the possibility of a drop in human birth rates as adults opt for having fewer children. Such a decline in births could potentially benefit the environment by reducing pressure on resources and mitigating some environmental impacts. A smaller population could lead to lower carbon emissions and reduced deforestation for farmland. However, some argue that, even with declining birth rates, unless there are also significant changes in consumption patterns and emissions reduction, the environmental benefits may not be guaranteed.

"We have no sense of what's coming," says planning professor Carlton Basmajian of Iowa State University. "Like a lot of questions, it's going to take a crisis or catastrophe before people start paying attention."

Every hundred or so years, humanity ponders how long it has to exist. Yet to date, the human race has somehow managed to replace itself, no matter what the threats. On the assumption that humans will continue to exist as a species into the next century and beyond, we have no choice but to live today believing that society has a future. And if it isn't too much to expect, a future of positive progress.

So, what happens to all those billions of human bodies over the next hundred or so years and beyond?

The primary aim of this book is to provide vital information that will help them make those decisions. The choice is up to the reader.

"If the universe is as many millions of years old as we think it is, this crowded little era is but an instant of yesterday when it is past. The one question remaining then, was it 23.59 o'clock or .0001? Was there to be still another cycle of affliction, appeasement, and annihilation, or had we walked through midnight towards the dawn without knowing it?" – Edward R. Murrow, 1945

Chapter 1: Water Cremation – New, Eco-Friendly and Affordable

"Every person who becomes liquid instead of ash would keep about 180 kilograms of carbon dioxide out of the atmosphere." – Independent Research Company TNO

"Alkaline hydrolysis is, in and of itself, a morally neutral action." – Sister Renée Mirkes, PhD, Franciscan Sisters of Christian Charity

---

Death care and the "industrial-commercial death-care complex," as it's come to be known, is overdue for change. That change is already underway.

On top of their responsibilities to their children, most adults are responsible for the care of their aging parents and managing the end of their lives, and then their own. Adding to the family burden: the rising cost of death.

The emotional impact related to death care is extremely stressful for many families, not to speak of the constantly increasing costs of dying, let alone living – one of the prime topics of this book (*see Chapter 13*).

Yet there are new answers to rising death costs. Recent technology can mean a significant easing of these costs, while reducing the impact on the Earth's fragile environment at the same time.

In the 19th century, there was only one option: burial. Then there were two.

Until the mid-1960s, casket burial was the only option for most in the West. That's when flame cremation started to become increasingly available and the popular choice, spurred in part by the Vatican's policy change in 1963 to lift its prohibition on cremation for Catholics under specific conditions. The Catholic Church has since relaxed its policies on cremation even further.

But now there's a third option.

The breakthrough came in the final decade of the 20th century when a new approach emerged involving, not flame cremation, but cremation by water. For those who are religious, as well as those who are not, saving the planet has become a tantamount concern for this and future generations.

The new method, called alkaline hydrolysis, was developed by doctors at Albany Medical College in New York in the early 1990s, about a century after it was first used for the disposal of farm animal bodies in England.

So, What Exactly is Alkaline Hydrolysis?

It's the scientific term for an ecologically friendly alternative to flame cremation. It's also known as aquamation, water cremation, or a number of other less-scientific terms: flameless cremation, green cremation, aqua-cremation, hydro-cremation, liquid cremation, aquamation, resomation, or simply 'AH.'

In short, it dissolves human remains at a fraction of the cost of flame cremation, with close to a tenth of the emissions.

In this process, decomposition is the same as that which takes place during burial, but is accelerated by chemicals. The body of the deceased person is sealed in a vessel, then a lye solution of 95 percent water and five percent potassium or sodium hydroxide is introduced at a moderate temperature (177°C or 350°F) that rapidly reduces soft tissue to its basic elements. Pressure or agitation is often used to promote decomposition, leaving only inorganic bone material, which is then dried and crushed. No tissue and no DNA are left after the process. The dry, white, powder-like remains are returned to the family.

According to the Cremation Association of North America, the sterile effluent that drains off is far cleaner than most wastewater. The effluent, made up of salts, sugars, amino acids, and peptides, much like liquid soap, must comply with federal, state or provincial, and local laws. Water treatment authorities generally like having the liquid enter the system because it helps clean the water as it flows back to the treatment plant. In some cases, the water is diverted and used for fertilizer because of the potassium and sodium content.

There are two approaches to alkaline hydrolysis. One uses a higher temperature/pressure system that processes the body at 320°F (160°C) at an elevated pressure, which prevents boiling and takes four to six hours. That's fast enough to process multiple bodies in one day.

The alternative is a low-temperature machine that processes the body at 208°F (98°C) over 14 to 16 hours.

High-pressure machines cost up to $500,000, significantly more than the $175,000 low-temp units.

The cost of alkaline hydrolysis, or aquamation, to the family typically falls between $2,000 and $5,000, but likely will soon come down with more systems available and wider acceptance by both the death care industry and by consumers.

Originated in Britain

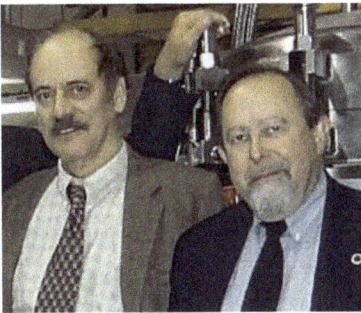

Drs. Peter Weber (left) and Gordon Kaye developed alkaline hydrolysis for human bodies in the 1990s.

The process was patented in 1888 by Englishman Amos Herbert Hobson for disposing of animal bodies. In 1992, Drs. Gordon Kaye and Peter Weber, colleagues at Albany Medical College in New York, revisited the method for accommodating human remains. Since then, the process has gradually but steadily become better known and continues to attract interest and public support.

Reached at age 90 at his home in Florida, where he retired, Dr. Weber recalled having lunch with the late Dr. Kaye one day in 1992 and sketching on a napkin the concept for the use of the method in human disposition. To a

8

suggestion by the author that the technology may someday soon revolutionize death care and eventually replace flame cremation, he responded, "I'll be very happy to see that."

The gentle process has been described as a body being 'bathed' in warm water. One web portal compares it to ice melting in a glass of water. With warm liquid around it, the ice gradually disappears.

"Alkaline hydrolysis or liquid cremation is a clean, green alternative to fire-based cremation, using only 10 percent of the energy and producing no air emissions," wrote Victoria Haneman, a former professor at Creighton University School of Law. "Existing law," she said, "is being leveraged to obstruct this innovative death technology from being more broadly available to consumers."

Many now increasingly see it as the logical default method for the disposition of human bodies. And some, including more and more funeral directors, predict it will replace flame cremation as the most eco-friendly and affordable process.

Independent Research Company TNO said, "Every person who becomes liquid instead of ash would keep about 180 kilograms of carbon dioxide out of the atmosphere," Scientific American Magazine reported in 2017.

Still, many don't realize such a method exists. For their own sake, it's time they found out.

The high cost of alkaline hydrolysis to date has been largely due to the cost of the machines to funeral homes. When lower-cost systems become more widely available, as is already happening, regulatory authorities will realize that their liquid emissions create virtually no impact on the environment. Many municipalities, in fact, acknowledge that the alkali can offset the acidity of their wastewater systems. The alkalinity encourages water molecules to dissolve the body. The prices are likely to come down as the process becomes more popular.

The effluent also breaks down residue from treatments like chemotherapy and other medications in the body, providing actual benefits to the environment. In addition, the technology is the single disposition method that eliminates prions that cause spongiform encephalopathy (mad cow disease). A 2019 U.S. study found the method did eliminate prion-sized particles.

Most in the death care field already know, or should know, about the process. Alkaline hydrolysis has been in use in the United States, Canada, the United Kingdom, and at least eight other countries for the disposition of human bodies since early 2005. But until recently, many consumers have remained unaware of this gentle, safe, affordable, and eco-friendly method of dealing with the dead.

However, as public demand grows and older equipment, especially retorts, requires replacement, it's likely that funeral homes will eventually have to invest in more alkaline hydrolysis technology.

Climate Change and 'The New Normal'

For many years, flame-based cremation was seen as more environmentally friendly than traditional casket burial, but incinerating the human body falls far short of being a non-pollutant. Due to the energy required and the impact it produces on the environment, particularly while global warming is a serious concern, the burning of bodies is a substantial source of air, land, and water pollution. And cremation by fire is far from gentle.

A study conducted by a university in the Netherlands examined green burial, flame cremation, and alkaline hydrolysis and their impacts. It concluded that green burial and alkaline hydrolysis have the lowest environmental impact. AH is a clean, green alternative, consumes a small percentage of the energy of flame cremation, produces no emissions from non-existent stacks, and uses no valuable land. It also accelerates the way the body decomposes, using heated water and lye.

The European Parliament approved the method precisely because it destroys prions that flame cremation does not.

The Cremation Association of North America (CANA), among others, agrees that alkaline hydrolysis is a gentler process than either flame cremation or casket burial, which has its own adverse environmental impact. It uses significantly less fuel and delivers less of a carbon footprint.

Barbara Kemmis,
Executive Director of the
Cremation Association of
North America

The association prefers the technical term 'alkaline hydrolysis' in place of trade names or euphemisms because it clearly describes what happens using water to break chemical bonds. It considers AH simply another form of cremation, said Barbara Kemmis, the association's executive director.

"The body goes in," she said, "bone fragments come out."

Laws Expanding to Permit the Process

As U.S. states and Canadian provinces began to legalize alkaline hydrolysis, their laws have redefined cremation to include both flame and water applications, Kemmis explained. The association recognized the trend and, in 2011, chose to agree that cremation is simply the process of speeding up decomposition, traditionally done with fire, but also through the chemical process of alkaline hydrolysis.

The broader definition includes any 'mechanical and/or thermal or other dissolution process that reduces human remains to bone fragments.'

"The association was the only trade organization to take this position," she said.

"Webster's Dictionary defines 'cremate' as reducing bodies to ashes by burning. Because alkaline hydrolysis doesn't burn, people claim it's not cremation. But cremation is not defined by dictionaries. It's defined in legislation.

Water cremation is also a smart choice from a business perspective, she told St. Louis Public Radio, pointing out that "flame cremation emissions come out of retort stacks," Kemmis said, adding, "It's also difficult for some businesses to get permission to place new cemeteries, particularly in urban areas. It's much easier to get zoning permission to put in an alkaline hydrolysis facility."

Minnesota was the first state to legalize the method in 2003. By 2025, aquamation had been legalized in 28 U.S. states, and bills were pending in Pennsylvania, Texas, and North Dakota.

The United Kingdom, Australia, Mexico, the Netherlands, and South Africa were also using the method. Largely Catholic Ireland introduced it in 2023.

In Canada, four provinces and one territory had authorized the method by 2025. The lone funeral home in Yellowknife, the largest community in the Northwest Territories (population 45,800), has been offering the option since 2020. The funeral director there, Janice McKenna, has had success with the method. "Much more than I thought," she said. "The process is very good."

More U.S. States Planning to Legalize

In 2024, Pennsylvania Assemblywoman Mary Jo Daley co-sponsored a bill to legalize the method. The bill was back in the Legislature in early 2025, where it had passed in 2024 by a vote of 138 to 63, but still required Senate approval as of this printing.

"More than 4 million gallons (15,143 cubic meters) of toxic embalming fluids and 20 million (board) feet (3.47 cubic kilometers) of wood are put in the ground in the U.S. every year (for traditional casket burials)," she and her co-sponsor pointed out. "A single flame cremation emits as much carbon dioxide as a 1,000-mile (1,600-kilometer) car trip," the assembly members wrote. Because nothing is burned during the alkaline hydrolysis procedure, no toxic gases or air pollutants are produced, they argued.

A similar bill before a Texas legislature committee was also expected to be reintroduced in 2025.

Legislation to legalize the process in New York State was defeated in 2012, but was expected to be introduced again by 2025. The number of deaths in the state reached just under 166,000 in 2023, an increase of more than 9,500 over five years.

Some other states and Canadian provinces are also contemplating broadening their definition of cremation to include aquamation.

"The struggle to broadly legalize the process of alkaline hydrolysis suggests the need for a new era of 'light-touch' regulation by state lawmakers regulating the death care industry or an approach by which the government stays out of the way to allow market forces to shape the marketplace," Victoria Haneman of Creighton University wrote in 2021. "The introduction of the method into the U.S. death care culture is no grassroots movement."

"North Carolina funeral director Scott Groce believes there will be an inevitable shift, and I think the price will come down, like happened with the cost of cremation retorts. When the price drops, sooner or later," he predicted, "the funeral home is going to say 'yes, this is the future'."

"There's a growing wave towards a more viable alternative to flame cremation," Groce said. He's been offering the greener alternative as a choice for families since 2023. "It's been slow to gain acceptance by both the public and by the funeral industry," he agreed. "But over time, aquamation, or alkaline hydrolysis, is simply going to grow and grow." And for those who've opposed the method, he said, "I don't think there's any way around it."

Groce has had the foresight, as has a growing number of others in the death care sector, to anticipate what's going to happen. "It's a field that's been resistant to new ideas," he acknowledged. "Funeral directors are notorious for not wanting to change. For these old funeral home guys, maybe myself included, change is tough. You kind of get used to the pattern of the way business is done."

"But it's the best thing for the environment," he said, "and it will become the predominant choice."

The National Funeral Directors Association has yet to take a position on AH, but Groce thinks it will soon encourage people to investigate it and encourage legislators to legalize the new method. The NFDA's interest is in protecting and educating the consumer to make good, informed, and reasonable choices and to "make sure funeral homes are doing so, as well."

But the association's role, he added, isn't about money. "They're in it for consumers to have options. These are choices that are more affordable."

Funeral directors, he forecast, will soon lobby legislators to "take a good, hard look at this and to have it as an option. It's a safe one and an environmentally friendly one," Groce said. "There's no reason for it not to be legal and an option for people in all 50 states."

Tutu's Influence

South African Archbishop, Nobel Laureate, and environmental champion Desmond Tutu

The late Anglican Archbishop Desmond Tutu led by example. Before his death at the end of 2021, Tutu, who stood against South Africa's apartheid regime and earned the Nobel Peace Prize for his defence of human rights, demonstrated his commitment to environmental protection by arranging the disposition of his body by an eco-friendly liquid method. "Dying people should have the right to choose how and when they leave Mother Earth," Tutu had said.

The fact that his body underwent the process at a service in Cape Town, South Africa, on New Year's Day, 2022, following his death from cancer, received wide international coverage. Revered for a lifetime of work for racial justice, the 90-year-old anti-apartheid champion wanted an environmentally friendly funeral, devoid of ostentation. Tutu's final wishes set a compelling example for anyone concerned about the planet.

"It was very influential," said Joe Wilson, the founding CEO of Bio-Response Solutions, which has manufactured aquamation machines since 2006 at his plant in Indiana.

The newer method may become acceptable to even the more conservative bishops of the Catholic Church, he believes, leading to endorsement of the technology, similar to what happened when Pope Paul VI lifted the ban on cremation in 1963.

Joe Wilson, founding CEO of Bio-Response Solutions

"It's going to put tremendous pressure on the Catholic Church," Wilson said, "because of the affiliations Tutu had with Christian doctrine and environmental protection." Some believe Tutu put the world on notice to choose an environmentally sound process, he added.

Resistance from American Catholic Bishops

The Catholic Church's permission of fire cremation, some point out, is a "grudging permission" that doesn't extend to water-based cremation. Many consider it 'troubling' that the Church is blocking safe and innovative death technology from becoming available for use by non-Catholics. Conservative Catholic bishops, representing a minority of the U.S. population, have apparently been influential in persuading several state governments to reject legislation authorizing alkaline hydrolysis.

In their effort at obstruction, the bishops are aligning themselves against a method of disposition that has a minimal impact on global warming. They're attempting to impose their views on state affairs while at the same time obstructing an affordable method for families. Advocates say the bishops have no authority over disposition decisions by non-Catholics or to influence state legislators on the matter. And elected representatives have a responsibility to their electorate to resist any attempts at pressure from outside groups.

The Funeral Consumers Alliance of Maryland and Environs, in a 2023 submission to the state senate finance committee, said, "A basic tenet of our democracy is the separation of church and state, and the Catholic Church should have no authority to decide for others what constitutes a dignified disposition."

Lack of Consensus Among Catholics

Although the bishops joined other religious lobbyists in opposing its legalization, there's a lack of consensus among Catholics. Just 21 percent of Americans in 2021 described themselves as Catholic, while 10 percent no longer were practicing members, citing a loss of belief, disenchantment, indifference, or affiliation with another religion.

As for some Catholic bishops opposing the method, consecutive popes have become more open to change in recent years and have "lessened their grip and made more choices available," North Carolina's Groce said.

Sister Renée Mirkes, PhD, of the Franciscan Christian Charity, director of the influential Center for NaProEthics, made an argument for the scientific advantages of the process in the National Catholic Bioethics Quarterly in 2008.

"The Catholic Church has sound theological reasons for its unswerving promotion of burial as the normative practice for bodily disposition," she wrote. "But given its environmental, geographical and public health advantages, predictions are that requests for alkaline hydrolysis, once the process is legalized, will rival and perhaps exceed current U.S. requests for (flame) cremation." One must consider, she continued, whether it would qualify 'in cases of necessity' as a moral alternative to Christian burial?"

Sister Renée Mirkes, Ph.D., Director, Center for NaProEthics

Her conclusion: "The process of alkaline hydrolysis is, in and of itself, a morally neutral action. When chosen for serious reasons, that is, out of necessity and in a way that confesses belief in the resurrection of the body, alkaline hydrolysis is a moral means of final bodily disposition."

Professor Philip Olson, a technology ethicist at Virginia Polytechnic Institute, realizes there's opposition to the process but said many people find it "perfectly acceptable, if not preferable" to the alternatives and that many Catholics are already accepting the science and benefits of alkaline hydrolysis.

"Some people will pay more for it," Olson said. "They think it's worth spending more to do something that's environmentally friendly."

The archdiocese of St. Louis has appeared more receptive if the method of disposing of the liquid effluent changes. The current practice of disposing of the liquid into water mains, it said, "violates the dignity of the deceased." Catholics should avoid it "until another suitable method of disposing of the liquid remnant can be established."

Experts, however, say the liquid is not harmful to the environment, going through the water treatment process, just as other liquid wastes do.

Some point out references in Christian, Jewish, and Muslim scriptures to purifying by water. In the Bible, purification by water is a common practice that involves washing the body or sprinkling with water. (Ephesians, Leviticus, Numbers). The rite of Levitical purification by water is a type of baptism.

The book of Ephesians refers to "the washing with water through the word" as a way to sanctify and cleanse. This phrase is often interpreted as referring to baptism and the spiritual cleansing that happens through the Word of God. While not explicitly stating that water washes away all sins, it does emphasize the cleansing and purifying nature of water within the context of the Christian faith. In the book of Acts, water represents the washing away of sins and the beginning of "a new life in Christ."

The phrase 'punishment by fire' is an ancient reference to the idea that those who don't repent from their sins will be punished by flames.

The 'Ick Factor'

"Another aspect of opposition to alkaline hydrolysis is the so-called 'ick factor,'" said the Cremation Association's Barbra Kemmis. "Some people think it's gross to dissolve bodies and disrespectful to 'flush grandma down the drain.'"

"Their misgivings, however, aren't based on the fact that alkaline hydrolysis does not use acid, and the wastewater does not contain 'bits of grandma,' especially compared to the wastes of embalming."

Those favouring the process say it's no more disrespectful than other forms of disposition, particularly flame cremation. Josh Slocum, former executive director of the Funeral Consumers Alliance, said there's nothing distasteful about it.

"Finding alkaline hydrolysis 'icky' has not a goddamned thing to do with whether it should be legal or not," Slocum said. "Effluent from the process discharged into sewers has no bearing on the issue. Funeral homes for years have been flushing all the blood, body fluids, formaldehyde, and formalin solutions into the sewers, yet have never been required to have a special license."

"What goes into the wastewater treatment system is probably cleaner than most things that go into the wastewater treatment system from our house or hospitals or nursing homes or other places," said John McQueen, a funeral director in St. Petersburg, Florida, where a Resomation unit was installed in 2011, one of the first in the United States to the offer the process.

Despite the opposition, alkaline hydrolysis is here to stay as a proven alternative technology for human disposition.

"It took 100 years for traditional cremation to reach five percent of dispositions in the United States," said Kemmis, who believes the process will find success on a much shorter timeline. "What's needed is improved public education and enough regulatory stability for funeral businesses to feel comfortable making the leap into this new technology."

"Whether they use high-temp or low-temp machines, advocates of alkaline hydrolysis agree it is an answer to the looming crisis over the disposition of millions of bodies and is preferable to cremation and ground burial," she added.

Sandy Sullivan launched Resomation Ltd. in Scotland in 2007.

"It's one answer," said biochemist Sandy Sullivan, who formed the UK-based Resomation Ltd. in Glasgow, Scotland, in 2007, building only high-pressure units. His process uses five times less energy than flame cremation and reduces greenhouse gases by 35 percent. Sullivan claims his technology is "a totally different beast" from the units sold in the United States, Canada, the Netherlands, and several other countries.

"It's good for society, it's good for the environment, and the quicker the backward ideas of the industry are resolved, the better," Sullivan told Wired Magazine. He said his equipment is three or four times as fast and produces a better "quality of ash" at the end of the process, benefits that he said justify the higher cost.

"I don't think it's going to be the be-all or end-all or a panacea to all the issues with flame cremation," he said, "but, like alternative energy, composting, and other ones that I don't even see on the horizon, it's all good. The more the merrier, and that means there's a quicker move away from flame cremation."

Added Sullivan's American rival, Joe Wilson at Bio-Response Solutions: "With all the deaths that are going to face our planet every day going forward, all the techniques better be considered and put into practice before the system gets overwhelmed."

The process is now viewed as the most eco-friendly and affordable option for families faced with the deaths of relatives, often sudden and unexpected.

Incineration-based cremation was considered more eco-friendly than traditional casket burial, but it falls far short of being ideal because of the energy consumed and air emissions produced.

"Opponents express concerns about public health and safety and about the dignity of our mortal remains," Olson of Virginia Polytech observed. "But proponents focus on its environmental benefits over flame cremation and earth burial, aligning the technology with the 'green burial' movement."

In 2005, the process was installed at the Mayo Clinic in Minnesota, where it was an option for donated human bodies. Two years later, more than 1,000 people had chosen it as their preferred method of disposition.

"Everything about this process is a win-win; everything is recyclable," Dr. Dean Fisher at the University of California in Los Angeles said in 2008, adding that 1,200 bodies had gone through UCLA's Resomator since it went into service in 2012. Haneman supports "absolutely everything" among innovative death care and disposition technologies, particularly liquid cremation, a clean, green alternative to fire-based cremation, using only 10 percent of the energy and producing no air emissions.

A growing number of funeral directors in the United States, Canada, and the UK are effusive about their benefits, both to grieving clients and to their own bottom lines.

Drew Gray, a now-retired funeral director in Prince Albert, Saskatchewan, was the first to offer alkaline hydrolysis in Canada. It became preferred by most of his customers. He initially intended to offer cremation, but zoning regulations wouldn't allow a crematory retort. That led him to Indiana, where he ended up buying a low-temp/low-pressure unit from Bio-Response Solutions, which had led the North American market.

Gray became a staunch advocate of the method. "We had a fantastic experience," he said. He was conducting as many as 100 funerals a year, soon after he started with alkaline hydrolysis, and the number was growing until he retired. Gray had even changed his own pre-arranged funeral to use the procedure.

"Why do we incinerate bodies anymore?" people asked Gray. "We're all looking for alternatives," he said. "Aquamation has a certain tastefulness factor. We have to make death as palatable as we can."

Chapter 2: Alkaline Hydrolysis – The Next Generation

"The future has already arrived." – William Gibson,
Essayist and Futurologist

Even newer technological advances will make alkaline hydrolysis available across North America and possibly abroad. Much sooner and more affordably than ever.

It will likely revolutionize death care.

And it comes from an improbable source: a small company in British Columbia, Canada, that's been producing electric control panels for 45 years. Company engineer Theo Nguyen had the original concept of revolutionizing the existing designs for aquamation equipment to produce machines that are both smaller and less expensive than those previously on the market.

"The concept is to make this affordable for small, independent funeral homes," said Stan Hussey, the owner of Harbourview Electric in Burnaby, BC, acknowledging that his company may be seen as revolutionary in the death care field. "That's what we're hoping to do. We think it is a really good solution for the whole world."

Operating under the name Aqualyser Solutions, his company will be producing less-intimidating units that look like large home freezers or refrigerator-shaped bathtubs.

At the time of publication, the plan was to sell the system for substantially less than the cost of other devices already on the market. The price the buying public pays would be far less than what's now charged. Welcome news to those coping with the growing challenges of funeral poverty. (*See Chapter 13*).

The company conducted numerous on-site tests of the system in the late fall of 2024 using donated human bodies at a funeral home in Oregon that already was using the alkaline hydrolysis system.

"All trials were a success," said Guy Heywood, one of Hussey's partners, approximating the results achieved by other systems in the past 10 years. "The difference is that the system is more affordable, takes less space, and is easy to operate," he added.

Guy Heywood (left) in an Aqualyser 'basket'
Stan Hussey (right) with the remains from the Aqualyser process

"The Aqualyser is a simple, uncomplicated design without the industrial look and feel or the noise and heat that comes from the typical gas-fired crematory," Heywood said.

"A large metal 'basket' is used to transfer the body into the machine, but there's a lot of science and trials that go into the exact design and the way it affects the fluid dynamics inside the vessel," he added. "The body handling system will be different in every user's facility. Some will be installed, starting from scratch in a purpose-built room, so the equipment for handling the body will depend on the height of the ceiling."

Nguyen has been working with funeral director Jon Hughes of St. Louis to make several small changes to the design of the vessel.

Hughes was already a firm believer in the value of alkaline hydrolysis when he met with Heywood in Burnaby and purchased an Aqualyser at a considerably lower price than the second-hand one he was using. At just one process per day, Hughes was already turning business away.

He had purchased the low-pressure unit in 2017 from Ohio funeral home director Jeff Edwards when that state's regulator wouldn't approve water cremation in his funeral home.

"It's going to be the coming thing," Hughes said. "I don't know how soon that will be, but I'm excited to see this happening. It's going to help the industry, particularly when the costs of the machines come down."

"With alkaline hydrolysis, there is no carbon output, no smoke, and no gas coming off the machines," he said. He predicts that, with the new process developed in British Columbia, the consumer price will drop as it becomes more popular.

Inventor and developer Theo Nguyen shows off the Aqualyser to St. Louis funeral director Jon Hughes, who bought a unit, and to Courtney Greewalt of Pearson's Funeral Home in Oregon.

Aqualyser executives (L–R) Guy Heywood, Stan Hussey, and Theo Nguyen welcome Sara Williams, president of the Funeral Consumers Alliance, to the Burnaby, B.C., office.

The price of alkaline hydrolysis to the consumer has normally been similar to flame cremation, between $1,200 and $1,600, but can be as high as $3,000 or as low as $600-700. Some funeral homes offer AH as a premium service. But with the new design originating in British Columbia, the price will drop as it becomes more accepted.

"It will cater to everyone," Heywood said. "In a society with increasing disparities of income and wealth, our bodies are all going to have the same state. Mortality is a common bond the rich have not yet managed to break, and greater awareness of that shared human truth could be a good thing.

"We don't want alkaline hydrolysis to become the preferred disposition of low-income populations," he stressed. "We want to be a positive choice made by every enlightened person, like Archbishop Tutu, who is self-aware and considerate of those they are leaving behind. We'll offer an affordable service, while maintaining a high level of care and professionalism in the way the Aqualyser will be used as part of the funeral service for every family, not focusing on a high volume of cases."

The market for a new AH product is opening up as funeral homes in the United States and Canada report that the demand for cremation, both flame and water, is growing. At the same time, their existing retorts and older water cremation machines are reaching capacity, are costly to maintain, or require replacement.

Aqualyser's stainless-steel vessels are fabricated in Salmon Arm, B.C, with the electrical, plumbing, and controls installed at Harbourview in Burnaby. Alternative manufacturing sites are also being considered at locations in the United States. A company in Ontario may be able to reduce the cost even more significantly.

While the Aqualyser is being manufactured in British Columbia, ironically, it cannot be used in the province. The BC government has been slow to legalize aquamation in spite of a petition urging it to do so, which would help Hussey's company develop a healthy new industry and jobs. The provincial government, narrowly re-elected in 2024, may be reconsidering its non-decision after prolonged delays. Hussey is reluctant to move out of British Columbia, but he will if necessary.

Chapter 3: The Death of the Cemetery?

"Casket embellishments are often made of plastic, metal, fabric, paint and varnish that contain chemicals that leach into the ground over time and contaminate soil, water and ecosystems." – The David Suzuki Foundation, an organization focused on environmental sustainability

For millennia, people have been burying their dead. They use elaborate caskets, sometimes simple coffins. Despite the growing popularity of cremation, the tradition of interring the deceased in a cemetery plot or even a crypt is conducted with ritual, tradition, and often religious meaning.

The standard procedure calls for removal/transfer of the remains to the funeral home, preparation of the body (including casketing, cosmetology, dressing, grooming and often embalming), a metal casket, use of facilities and staff for viewing and funeral ceremony, use of a hearse, use of a service car/van, and a basic memorial printed package, like memorial cards and register book.

The cost doesn't take into account cemetery, monument, or marker costs, the price of a vault, or miscellaneous cash-advance charges such as for flowers or an obituary.

Funeral homes in the U.S. must also accept a casket that has been purchased online.

The Federal Trade Commission's Funeral Rule regulates the funeral trade in the United States. Canada, the United Kingdom, and New Zealand have similar regulations dealing with the treatment of bodies.

Many funeral directors insist, erroneously and deliberately, that embalming is either required by law, necessary to protect the health of the public, or a religious requirement. They recommend it for disinfection, preservation, restoration, and identification, which is unnecessary since most bodies come from a medical facility and have an identification wristband. Funeral homes can't embalm a body without written consent. Some require embalming if there is to be a public viewing, but cannot require it for private family services.

The embalming process starts with washing the body with disinfectants. Then the blood is replaced with preservative fluids, often formaldehyde-based chemical solutions. Finally, the internal organs and cavities will be drained and injected with another chemical mixture. Embalming also involves manipulation of the limbs so they can be easily positioned and the face to ensure it holds its shape during visitation.

Embalming is used less frequently today because refrigeration is at least as effective and doesn't require chemicals or invasive procedures. It had become a common practice during the Civil War in the United States when bodies of soldiers needed to be preserved to be shipped home. With few exceptions, today it is strictly for profit.

"That's a $600 fee," said Canadian death care coach Stephen Garrett, "and it's not necessary." In British

Columbia, the government has declared that embalming serves no useful purpose in preventing the spread of communicable disease.

The FTC Funeral Rule states that embalming is not required by law, except in special cases. In most states, health codes do not require embalming, and some states only require it in certain circumstances.

Embalming is considered desecration by Muslims, Orthodox Jews, and the Bahá'í faith. It has no basis in Christianity.

Caskets and Burial Vaults

Equally contentious, from considerations of both money and utility, are the containers, usually made of concrete or steel, that enclose a coffin to help prevent a grave from sinking or, worse, caving in.

Traditional coffins are anything but green. Expensive coffins are built so they won't decompose. Casket burials, in most cases, use hazardous chemicals and non-biodegradable materials. The cheaper ones are made of plastic and fiberboard. The glue used for fiberboard coffins is a pollutant, often containing formaldehyde. Cemeteries are often ecologically barren due to herbicide and fertilizer use.

In most of North America, many cemeteries and funeral homes insist on the use of a burial vault or grave liner, though not legally required. Funeral directors often try to sell the costliest vault they have, with the highest profit margins. Their use is declining as cremation numbers rise. Which is probably just as well because the vaults don't allow for decomposition, which is their whole point.

Professor Carlton Basmajian of Iowa State University

Professor Carlton Basmajian of Iowa State University says the materials used to build them, especially concrete, are notoriously environmentally unfriendly. Alterations to the landscape, he says, are made both above ground, where insecticides and herbicides are often applied, and below ground, where there's concrete, metal, and toxic chemicals (in the embalmed body). Natural or green burials don't use a casket at all, which means minimal settling.

It's estimated that traditional burials in the United States use 20 million board feet (3.47 cubic kilometers) of wood a year, plus 4.3 million gallons (16.3 million liters) of embalming fluid, 1.6 million tons (1.45 million metric tons) of reinforced concrete, 17,000 tons (15,400 metric tons) of copper, and 64,500 tons (58,500 metric tons) of steel.

David Charles Sloane's 2018 book *Is the Cemetery Dead?* raised legitimate questions about conventional ground burial, pointing out that cemeteries can be wasteful and harmful in terms of land use and materials, with chemicals, plush caskets, and manicured greens adding to the problem. Research has found that conventional ground burial causes serious environmental contamination.

Sloane suggested these factors threaten the future of cemeteries and may lead them to become more environmentally responsive.

Groundwater Contamination

Studies on the impact of cemeteries on groundwater quality brought wide agreement among scientists that cemeteries produce hazardous emissions. Each kilogram of a decomposing human body produces contaminated liquid that contains pathogenic bacteria and viruses that may "contaminate the groundwater and cause disease when used for drinking," researcher Józef Żychowski wrote in 2015. The leachate also includes mineral salts, organic chemicals, and metallic compounds, including calcium, chromium, iron, manganese, and lead.

Embalming is also a source of metal pollution, resulting in the leaching of formaldehyde, potassium nitrate, chromium, and arsenic. Substances used in chemotherapy, prostheses, and dental implants also contaminate the ground.

By mid-2022, research had shown that COVID-19-related deaths were overfilling some cemeteries and increasing the leakage of metal pollution from graves. "The contamination of groundwater can have not only health and environmental impacts but also serious social and economic consequences," Żychowski said.

There's a significant threat to funeral home employees as well as people and animals living near cemeteries. Some studies have found high levels of bacteria in wells near burial grounds. The contamination can also reduce the quality of farming and agricultural products and leave water unsuitable for certain industrial processes and recreation. The threat is especially high in cemeteries located in low-lying lands that are flood-prone.

"Once water logs a cemetery," Basmajian said, "it becomes a huge problem that's going to get people's attention."

This is another problem expected to get worse with climate change.

Chapter 4: The End of Flame Cremation?

"Cremation takes up about the same amount of energy and has the same emissions as about two tanks of gas in an average car." – Nora Menkin, Former Executive Director of the People's Memorial Association

Cremation is the most popular and, at least for now, among the least costly methods of body disposition, but despite its green reputation, it's not environmentally friendly, though it does reduce land use.

"When discussing the 'cremation of bodies,' the most relevant term regarding environmental impact would be 'emissions,' as cremation processes release airborne pollutants like carbon monoxide, particulate matter, and potentially harmful chemicals like mercury," ScienceDirect.com says.

Families may choose to emulate a traditional burial service, with the body transferred to a crematory after a service. A special casket for viewing may be rented for this purpose. Or they may opt for direct cremation, followed by whatever service the family wishes or none at all.

The burning of bodies is a significant source of air, land, and water pollution. Fossil fuels are used to fire the crematorium, usually heated by propane- or butane-fueled burners. Cremation in a gas crematory (or retort) involves combustion, vaporization, and oxidation of the body into gas, ashes, and mineral compounds.

Green burial advocate Mary Nash said people need a better understanding of what cremation does in terms of environmental damage before making their choice. People have told her that they're going "green," they're going to be cremated.

"You have to disillusion them and tell them, no, that's not going green," Nash said. "It's about the worst thing you can do. Cremation is pretty bad."

The preference for flame cremation over burial has significantly increased since the late 20th century and has led to the installation of new crematoria or the expansion of existing facilities. By 2035, the flame cremation rate is forecast to reach 80 percent in several countries, unless readily available eco-friendly alternatives become widely adopted.

During the cremation, the body is exposed to temperatures of up to 1,800°F (871–982°C). This process, on average, uses an equivalent of 28 gallons (106 liters) of fuel to cremate a single body and produces an estimated 545 pounds (247 kilograms) of carbon dioxide emissions.

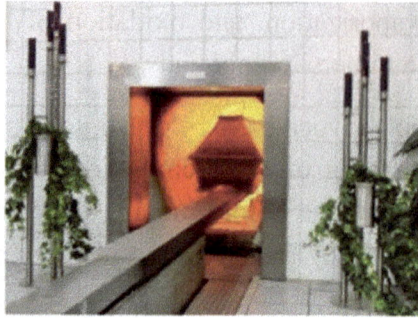

Flame cremation is now the preferred method of disposition in many industrialized countries, but it is not the eco-friendly solution many believe it to be.

The impact of pollution from cremation must be considered, as many millions are projected to die over the next 20 to 50 years. If the largest percentage of Americans choose cremation, that will add up to an equivalent of more than 1.4 billion gallons (5.3 billion liters) of fossil fuels burned and 27.5 billion pounds (12.5 billion kilograms) of carbon dioxide produced in the U.S. alone in that period.

How Cremation Works

There is no aesthetically pleasing way of disposing of human remains, Darryl J. Roberts, a 30-year veteran of the death care business, pointed out in his 1997 book, Profits of Death. (The late Lisa Carson, onetime executive director of the Funeral Ethics Organization, once said about Roberts, "There is no better person to blow the whistle in the funeral industry.")

"The application of the intense heat of cremation first evaporates the water from the body," Roberts wrote. "The flames then incinerate the muscles, flesh, and organs. Most of the bone structure will crumble, but will not be reduced to 'ash' by cremation.

"The actual incineration process takes an average of one to two hours, depending on the temperature inside the retort, the condition and size of the corpse (the bodies of obese individuals give off considerable black smoke and flames when incinerated and take longer than more slender folks), and the type of container used," he continued.

"Once the process is complete and the oven has cooled, an attendant removes the ashes and bone fragments using a brush similar to that used to clear pizza ovens," Roberts added (with an added apology to all pizza lovers). Sometimes a vacuum cleaner is used. The funeral industry uses the euphemism 'cremains' to refer to the ashes. These 'cremains' are placed in a box or in an urn purchased by the family.

If the ashes are to be scattered, they will probably be passed through a pulverizing machine to grind the bones. What results has the granular consistency of sand and bears no resemblance at all to human remains. In the pulverization process, Roberts wrote, it's inevitable that some residue from other cremains will be mixed in with others, and some of the cremains will be lost, but they're likely to be minuscule.

Before cremation, funeral homes remove pacemakers since they can explode. Titanium hip replacements, which tarnish but don't melt, are also usually removed as they can damage bone grinders. Otherwise, metal remnants such as pins, screws, and joints surgically placed in the body are separated out of the remains, usually with strong magnets, before the bones are ground.

Clothing for the deceased is optional. If there has been a traditional funeral, the bodies are cremated in their clothing. When there's a direct cremation without a service or viewing, they're cremated in whatever they passed away in, pajamas or a hospital gown, or a sheet. A corrugated box is used with a piece of plywood at the bottom to give it some strength.

Most requests for permission to witness a cremation are denied.

Environmental Impacts

Living near a crematorium can be dangerous because of air pollution from the cremation process. The health risks include damage to the brain, kidneys, lungs, heart, and even adverse birth outcomes. The World Health Organization and the U.S. Environmental Protection Agency advise that care be taken to limit exposure, particularly to vulnerable populations such as infants, children, pregnant women, and the elderly.

Smoke from a cremation retort in operation

"The environmental impact depends on the type of facility in which the cremation takes place," said Laura Green, senior toxicologist at Green Toxicology in Brookline, Massachusetts.

"The typical crematory in the U.S.," she said, "has until recently been part of a funeral home with one or two retorts. The primary emissions are carbon dioxide and fine soot, but sulphur dioxide and trace metals may also be produced."

"Larger, more sophisticated operations will funnel cremation after-gases into wet scrubbers or very large filters to reduce emissions. These methods can't eliminate all pollutants, but they are minimized to the point of being inconsequential," Green said. Smaller facilities are equipped with cyclone systems to control pollution, she adds, but they only deal with particulates, leaving combustion gases untreated.

The design of the retort, the height of the exhaust stacks, and the way in which the crematory is operated will also influence the amount of pollution it produces.

"Like all things, there are good ones and bad ones," Green said. "Whether there should be better federal regulations is a good question."

Given the demand for cremation services, new crematoria need to be built and existing facilities expanded. In North America, crematories are regulated at the state, provincial, or territorial level. Most local governments permit crematoria in conjunction with cemeteries or in specified industrial zones, with minimum distances separating them from schools, daycares, libraries, and care facilities. But not all jurisdictions dictate and enforce setback distances, leaving the siting of a crematorium to the discretion of local officials.

That leaves municipalities answering questions about health risks to their residents, who generally oppose crematories anywhere near where they live.

There are few studies of how their emissions affect local air quality and whether they have an impact on local health. Some countries have set specific air pollution regulations for emissions of pollutants from crematoria, using ambient air quality criteria for identifying pollutants, but attributing emissions to a single source is not always accurate.

What Happens to the Ashes?

Of course, Funeral homes offer a wide variety of urns for the ashes of the deceased. People often choose to take the urn home and place it in a special spot.

Another option is committing the storage of the urn to a cemetery which has a columbarium, a room or building with niches where funeral urns can be placed.

Or, of course, you could scatter the ashes in a meaningful location, accompanied by a scattering ceremony where local regulations allow. Since they're sterile, it's a safe choice. You can even choose an urn already equipped with an organic medium that supports plant growth to mix with the ashes.

There are no prohibitions on scattering ashes on one's own land, provided it doesn't impact adjacent land use or streams. Some cemeteries permit scattering. Elsewhere, the landowner's permission should be sought. However, some state and provincial regulations prohibit scattering in some areas. While scattering at sea is permitted, there are federal regulations.

Green burial advocate Ed Bixby said there are more eco-friendly ways to dispose of a body than cremation. But he recognizes that, for many families, it's the affordable option.

"We realize that individuals and their families have to make hard decisions, and that sometimes comes down to dollars and cents, and they have to choose cremation," Bixby said. "We're saying that we can't advocate cremation, but if you opt for cremation, you've done what you need to do, and we respect that."

Green burial advocate, Ed Bixby

Chapter 5: Body Donation – 'The Kindest Gift'

"Mortui Presumes Vitae" ("Even in death do we serve life") – Inscription on a communal grave of donors, Bremgarten Cemetery, Switzerland.

It's called "the last best thing people can do."

The donation of human bodies for research is regarded by the medical community as the greatest gift anyone can make. Individuals and families are encouraged to consider full body donation as the most compassionate alternative to conventional burial when the time comes for this crucial decision, at or before the time of death. The objective is to advance medical and scientific knowledge.

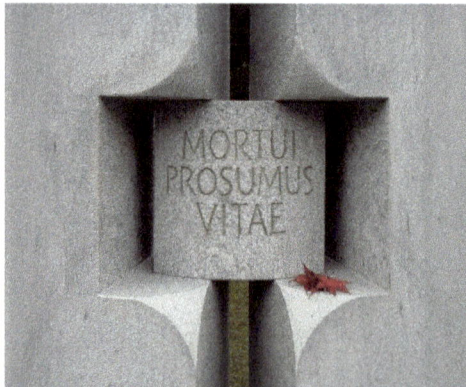

In most countries, body donations must follow state, provincial, or local laws. Donors should also be aware that the process of donation varies from country to country and state to state. A medical institution may have additional requirements, but it can't have fewer than those dictated by law. Consent for donation is provided by completing forms for the purpose available from any school of anatomy or orally in the presence of witnesses prior to death.

How to Register for Body Donation

Usually, one must register with the closest university medical school's 'anatomical gift' program. In the United States, close to 20,000 bodies a year are donated this way. Donation forms can vary among institutions. The next of kin may be required to give consent after death. The gifting of bodies to legitimate medical science has obvious value. But, in the strictest sense, however, it's not considered disposition. Donated bodies are not used indefinitely.

The study of the human body is one of the first and most important courses in the education of physicians. The study of anatomy serves as the foundation for training in surgery, pathology, and physiology. Surgeons often practice clinical procedures on human cadavers. Donations benefit kinesiology students, physical and occupational therapists, and even engineers. Bodies are also useful to researchers in pursuit of medical advances that will impact current and future generations.

"The need for specimens at university medical schools has remained consistent for years," said Dr. Ann Zumwalt, associate professor of anatomy at Boston University. "There's an amazing payoff for the students who have gone through the anatomy lab experience," she said.

Bodies for study and research are fixed or prepared and usually embalmed with formalin. Some schools use other techniques to maintain a body's lifelike qualities. Plastination is a process to preserve bodies or body parts, making it possible for students to conduct dissections without the odor of formalin. Physical fixation can be performed by freeze drying, though few schools use that method.

For students of anatomy, recent donations of new technology have been invaluable. Ultrasound for clinical imaging, monitors, and cameras allows entire classes to simultaneously visualize the anatomical structures of living subjects or donors.

New virtual dissection tables, called 'anatomages,' let students view the body without chemicals and smells from cadavers. "It's the most advanced 3D visualization system for anatomy and physiology being adopted in the world's leading medical schools," Zumwalt explained. "There are lots of things you can do with these tools."

Every donation is used to train as many people as possible, many of whom will go on to practice for three to four decades.

"It's fundamental to what they do," said Dr. Edwin Moore, head of the University of British Columbia's anatomy school. "Every donation is going to impact the health and well-being of thousands of people in the coming years. It's important they know how valuable that donation was."

Universities, palliative care centers, and nursing homes reinforce the significance of body donor programs. Funeral homes also explain the option of donating bodies for teaching and research. And many physicians and nurses set examples by donating their bodies to anatomical research.

A donated body must be approved by an ethics committee, and students must adhere to a code of professionalism. "Students learn from the anatomy, but they also learn from the humanity of it," Zumwalt said.

Dr. Ann Zumwalt, associate professor of anatomy at Boston University, working with students

The procedure is obviously different from dissecting an animal, she explained. Students very much think about donors as once-living human beings, not mere specimens for study. "They're growing as future doctors, and they're thinking about death and dying," she said. "They're thinking about who this person was."

It's sometimes hard cutting into that person, remembering their humanity, but the students also appreciate the need to "get the job done."

The supply of willed bodies in medical education and research has fortunately kept up with the increasing demand, although some schools have an easier time than others meeting the need for cadavers. Voluntary donations are more than enough for some, wrote Boston College law professor Ray Madoff. "This is particularly true for the most prestigious institutions, some of which have a surplus of cadavers and thus have stringent requirements for donation."

But lesser-known institutions often struggle to meet their need for bodies, and that's where anatomy legislation helps to make more available, Madoff explained. Those institutions may apply to prisons and hospitals to donate unclaimed bodies, which they would otherwise bury or cremate.

There are also limitations on what donations anatomy labs can accept. Anatomy schools can't consider prospective donors who have died of a transmissible disease. Donated bodies are embalmed by the schools, which are concerned about the health of their embalmers. Bodies that have undergone recent surgery, with open incisions or unhealed scars, and the extremely overweight are ineligible.

Many labs don't accept donors under a certain age, though anatomy schools often accept donations from parents of very young children, even neonatal infants and stillborn fetuses. Medical schools are not inclined to accept a body if the immediate family withholds consent.

Disposition of Donated Bodies

"Bodies donated for medical research are not kept indefinitely. How long a body is retained depends on what

49

it's used for," said Dr. Bruce Wainman of McMaster University's anatomy program in Hamilton, Ontario. If it's for a surgical skills course, it may be for weeks or months.

Once an institution has used the body for study, it is usually cremated, and an annual ceremony is held in recognition of the donations. The ashes are then returned to the families.

Zumwalt said that memorial ceremonies or 'services of gratitude' are held annually at all anatomy schools to honor each year's donors and are attended by their family members.

"We pay a lot of attention to the people who are the donors and their families," she stressed. Every medical school where she's worked is aware of this.

Anatomy labs at the Mayo Clinic in Minnesota and universities in Florida, California, and Texas allow the families of donor bodies to choose between alkaline hydrolysis and conventional cremation.

"Some families want the body returned for earth burial," said Shaun Heath, the Mayo's former anatomical services director. The scope of the Mayo Clinic's work means people come from the contiguous United States and from all over the world for medical care.

Organ Donations

Donation of human organs is also a profoundly selfless act, at least when done legitimately. The organ or tissue is removed in a sterile surgical procedure and transplanted into a recipient whose organ has failed or been damaged by disease or injury. A procurement organization determines the medical suitability of a donation based on the donor's medical history and age. The recipient will not know the donor's identity.

People of all ages should consider themselves potential donors, as the need for organs is far greater than the number of donors. Families can also choose to donate a relative's body or organs.

In most cases, donors can still have an open casket funeral. It is nevertheless important to discuss the impact of donating specific organs and tissues on the viewing with a recovery professional, who works with the funeral director to address such concerns.

Individuals who wish to be organ donors can join a donor registry, providing legal consent for the anatomical gift of organs, tissue, and eyes (these choices are often included with a driver's license); register at any time by filling out a Document of Gift form; sign and carry an organ donor card; let family members and loved ones, a healthcare provider, lawyer, or religious leader know of your wish to be a donor.

"The human body is the most complex system ever created," as business magnate and philanthropist Bill Gates has observed. "The more we learn about it, the more appreciation we have for what a rich system it is."

Few acts contribute to that learning more than the donation of a body, in whole or in part, to medical science.

Beware of Body Brokers

Fears of body snatchers may be a thing of the distant past

or of horror movies, but concerns about 'funeral poverty' remain. So does the potential for fraud and exploitation in such schemes. There is a great deal of confusion about the sale of human organs and entire bodies for profit.

Demand for organ transplants far exceeds organ availability. It is estimated that legal transplants performed address the needs of only 10 percent of all patients on waiting lists worldwide. As a result, thousands of people die every year waiting for a procedure.

A report from the Economics, Resources and International Affairs Division of the Canadian government said that the desperate need for organ transplantation surgeries has given rise to a lucrative, transnational criminal enterprise that enables organ seekers to purchase organs from donors. This enterprise, commonly referred to as organ trafficking, is a global phenomenon, the report said.

Anatomy laboratories caution families against being victimized by companies buying and selling their relatives' bodies to save them the costs of disposition or, in some cases, for gain.

Research indicates that illegal organ trade is on the rise, with a recent report by Global Financial Integrity estimating that the illegal organ trade generates profits between $600 million and $1.2 billion per year, with a span over many countries.

Illegally trafficked organs are very expensive. According to some reports, the cost of a kidney, the most commonly trafficked organ, can range from $50,000 (USD) to $120,000.

Purchasers are normally wealthy persons from developed nations. Because the purchase is generally conducted through a vast network that includes a broker who acts as an intermediary between the organ buyer and seller, a local recruiter, as well as medical professionals and local hospitals performing the illicit organ removal, very little money is left for the donor, the report said.

Victims are commonly from poor and vulnerable populations in developing countries. Many are reported to have been misled, coerced, or otherwise forced into selling their organs. The still-unregulated market for human bodies or body parts often borders on the obscene, reminiscent of 19th-century grave-robbing.

Organ trafficking remains a pervasive problem in many parts of the world. Attempts to prevent and prohibit it have experienced limited success. The challenge is that many countries, including Canada, do not explicitly prohibit travelling abroad for organ transplantation surgeries that have been organized through illicit means. Thus far, legislative attempts in Canada to strengthen federal laws relating to organ trafficking have been unsuccessful.

The body trade ostensibly has developed in recent years to increase the availability of human cadavers for research. Operators sell cadavers, or parts of them, without the full knowledge or informed consent of donors. The activity of most of these brokers is clearly unethical and, in some cases, criminal.

The Reuters news agency reported that each year, thousands of Americans donate their bodies in the belief that they are contributing to science. Many are unwittingly contributing to commerce, their bodies traded as raw material in a largely unregulated national transplant industry.

Body brokers are also known as non-transplant tissue banks, distinct from the organ and tissue transplant industry, which the U.S. government closely regulates, Reuters reported. It's regrettably and surprisingly easy to buy and sell human body parts in the United States.

Lawyers and governments say the sale and shipment of whole human body parts is legal in most states. While selling organs for transplant is illegal, selling parts donated for research or education is generally permitted. Few state laws offer oversight, and almost anyone, regardless of expertise, can dissect and sell human remains. No federal law regulates the sale of cadavers or body parts for research or education, though the FTC's Funeral Rule requires funeral homes to make certain disclosures to consumers.

There have been numerous reports of body brokers selling parts of or entire human bodies for profit, causing devastating grief to families over disrespect to their deceased loved ones. Most of the reports about body parts have resulted in either legal charges or class action suits by outraged families, many of them victimized by selling bodies to these buyers. There are reports of partnerships between body brokers and cash-strapped funeral homes, which can result in significant revenues.

"They really strongly advertise to get people to donate under false pretenses," said Dr. Thomas Champney of the University of Miami, Florida, one author of a 2019 report from the National Library of Medicine that decried the "commercialization or commodification" of willed bodies in programs that generate profit. "They can make it sound very noble and altruistic to get donors, then chop them up and sell them for various prices."

"There are also well-known cases of kickbacks from funeral homes," Champney agreed. "There's a lot of shady dealings in that regard. More education of the general public is needed to counter these companies' ability to prey on people's ignorance," he said.

Medical school anatomy programs don't consider it ethical to advertise. "We don't think it's appropriate to go to hospitals and funeral homes and strong-arm people into donating bodies," Champney said. "We put ourselves at a disadvantage, but I think it's the right thing to do."

If a family is looking to save on funeral and cremation costs, there are legitimate ways to donate a body without relying on body brokers. Reputable university medical programs can be trusted to provide respectful methods of disposition and a legitimate benefit to the science of medicine and the training of medical professionals.

" If people do really want to donate their loved one, there are other alternatives which are much more ethical and much more moral," Champney said.

But it's difficult to know exactly who you're donating to and where your body will end up. In some states with central anatomical boards, a person would donate a body to a clearing house for bodies, which then allocates cadavers or parts.

" I would hate for people to see the word 'medical' and think it's all the same thing," Dr. Ann Zumwalt said of the clearing houses. "The tricky thing is that in the U.S., the federal laws are relatively loose and state laws vary widely in how strict they are."

As a result, it is possible to accidentally donate bodies to companies that use donated cadavers for reasons other than legitimate medical ones.

There appears to be a general idea in the United States, said Champney, "Once you're dead, you're property. You have no more rights than an old refrigerator. As soon as an individual dies, if you want to do research on them, there are no rules or regulations."

Chapter 6: Green Burial – A Choice to Do No Harm

"It's a choice to add value to the earth in our death." – Ann Hoffner in Natural Burial Cemetery Guide.

═══════════════════════════════════════

Oona Mills knew just what to do when her grandmother died in 2018. "She was a natural gardener for most of her life and lived very minimally," she told The Guardian newspaper, "so it seemed very fitting for her to have a natural service, especially since she'd told me that the greatest achievement in her life was the compost that she'd made. Mills' woodland service aimed to keep the burial as low-tech as possible, using a wicker coffin and no embalming fluids."

"Natural burials are very effective," she said. "You can bury someone at three feet (1 meter) rather than six feet (1.8 meters) under, which is much quicker for the body to decompose."

Green burials are seen by proponents as a way to end our lives with an act of kindness to the environment.

In a nutshell, it means the body must be in its natural state to permit natural decomposition. Also known as natural burial, it's considered an eco-friendly alternative to burial in a wooden, metal, or concrete casket, 6 feet (1.8 meters) down in a conventional cemetery.

Advocates strive to live their lives in harmony with nature by enabling the natural processes of decay, seeing themselves dying as they lived.

Green burial proponents advocate for minimal impact on the environment.

While awareness is growing, many are still unfamiliar with the possibilities. One study by researchers at universities in Kansas and Manitoba discovered that half of the people over 60 who were environmentally active didn't know what natural or green burial involves.

In an introduction to her cemetery guide, journalist Ann Hoffner wrote that the movement weighs the consequences of its actions on the world. "It's a choice to do no harm and it's a choice to add value to the earth in our death," Hoffner said, adding that it can secure land in its natural state for years to come.

Many believe green burial was how Americans buried their dead until the 1860s Civil War in the United States, when modern embalming techniques were developed. "But modern green or natural burials have a different emphasis," she wrote. "It is a deliberate choice, an option to conventional burial."

There's much debate over the use of the word 'green' when discussing interment and ideas about what qualifies as a natural disposition. Broadly speaking, a burial ground can be considered green if it meets the following criteria:

- Caring for the dead with minimal environmental impact that aids in the conservation of natural resources.
- Reduction of carbon emissions.
- Protection of worker health.
- Restoration and preservation of natural habitats.

More particularly, green burials involve nothing in the way of formaldehyde embalming, concrete burial vaults, or varnished mahogany caskets. Many green burial advocates choose a biodegradable casket or simply a shroud made of a natural fiber. If a casket shell is used, it must be made primarily from reclaimed, recycled, or renewable materials that are biodegradable under burial conditions. Wicker, bamboo, and cardboard are options. Casket liners, fasteners, and handles must also be made from material acquired in an eco-sustainable manner. The coffin must be produced in a sustainable manner that conforms to fair trade practices. These can be purchased far in advance and are easily stored.

Graves are located a safe distance from drinking water sources. Markers may be natural fieldstones or none at all. Often, there is no need to use heavy equipment for burial in a green cemetery: the grave is part of reclaimed land or forest.

Greenhouse gas emissions produced by the transportation of the coffin and the body should be offset by environmentally friendly measures.

"If you're going down green," said Susan Greer of the Natural Burial Association in Canada, there is no tombstone or freshly mown grass treated with pesticides. "The planet's in trouble. Everything we do matters," she said, "in life, and as it turns out, in death."

For those who wonder, animals haven't caused a problem for natural burials. In more than 20 years, there has been no sighting of animals disturbing a natural grave. Their 18-24 inch (45-60 centimeter) depth is enough to discourage their interest.

Natural as well as hybrid cemeteries (offering both natural and conventional interment) that follow these practices fall under the general category of green cemeteries. Also covered are conservation burials, which are natural interments on conservation lands. Groups in the United States, the United Kingdom, Canada, Australia, and New Zealand are buying up land to conserve it for nature and human body disposition.

How Green is Green?

Death care consultant Shane Neufeld, who's managed, been employed by, or owned funeral homes for more than 30 years, said that the term "green burial" needs to be more clearly defined. It is in danger of becoming a "buzzword" and "a bit contrived."

Being buried without a casket or embalming could be where being green ends, he suggested. Purists want to take the definition of green burial further and outlaw fossil fuels, which, strictly speaking, would rule out transporting the body to the burial site by automobile.

"Do you ask your friends to pick up a shovel, or will you use a backhoe that uses diesel fuel?" asked Neufeld. "There's nothing green about a backhoe, but digging a grave is hard work that can take up to four hours. Families need to decide what they believe reasonably constitutes a green burial and just how natural they want to be."

However, if the grave is dug by hand, an experienced gravedigger must be in charge and provide a safety overview and proper equipment for the diggers. If a backhoe is used, the operator must be experienced, and the area restricted to the operator and qualified assistants.

Ed Bixby is a leader in the natural burial movement. The former president of the Green Burial Council in the United States, Bixby, resigned in 2023 to become a leader in founding the new Global Green Burial Alliance. "In death," he said, "you should still be able to care for your loved one and in a way that feels like they belong to you."

Bixby especially advises families to memorialize their loved ones by planting trees. "The best way I can explain that is, if you were to plant an oak tree, which has a very long life," he said, "what would the carbon offset of that tree be? If it were fortunate to live for more than 500 years, that carbon offset would erase the carbon footprint not only of the cremation but of the life that individual has lived."

Availability is Growing

By one recent count, the U.S. has more than 90 registered green burial cemeteries and memorial woodlands, regarded as natural burial sites. There are many more hybrid cemeteries.

Cemeteries offering green burial in the United States are listed in the Natural Burial Cemetery Guide. While not endorsing one cemetery over another, it helps readers make informed decisions. Regularly updated, the guide can be ordered from the site greenburialnaturally.org. Or one can go to nhfuneral.org for an up-to-date list of green and hybrid cemeteries in the U.S. and Canada.

Most Canadian provinces or territories permit green burial. There are 12 certified green burial sites in four Canadian provinces: British Columbia, Alberta, Ontario, and Nova Scotia. Until recently, only two provinces had full green-burial sites, nine of them in BC.

"We're trying to build awareness that it's legal," said Susan Greer, "because a lot of people think it isn't."

"People need options at the end of life", she added. "There are limits to how many bodies conventional cemeteries can hold, and if cremation is seen as the only alternative, it becomes a carbon pollution issue. People don't know that cremation is so eco-unfriendly, so we try to build awareness of that."

"There's no legal requirement in Canada to use a vault. However, some Canadian cemetery bylaws insist that a vault be used," Greer said, "which disqualifies them as natural burial options. Green burial can also be more costly in

Canada as a result of some restrictive cemetery regulations – something that needs to change."

In the United Kingdom, almost 300 sites are designated as natural burial grounds, the first of which opened in 1993. The Association of Natural Burial Grounds in the United Kingdom, created in 1994 to help people establish sites for green burial, provides guidance to natural burial ground operators and a code of conduct for members. One of its provisions requires that families be allowed to organize funerals themselves without the services of a funeral director if they wish. Choices available to the family range from simply wrapping the body in a shroud before it's interred to organizing a memorial service.

Increased Demand for Natural Burial

A survey by the National Funeral Directors Association in the United States found that almost 54 percent of Americans are considering green burial. More than 70 percent of cemeteries report an increased demand for natural burial.

Cost is one factor driving the demand. Burial in a green cemetery or natural preserve can cost, on average, $1,000 to $3,000, including the plot, opening and closing of the grave, and a one-time fee for perpetual care. For a burial plot in Canada, it's often closer to $4,500.

A natural plot in a hybrid cemetery is generally the same price as a conventional plot, but the savings on embalming, coffins, and vaults can run over $8,500.

As for the environmental cost, a green burial, over a normal 50-year cycle, produces about as much carbon as driving an average car for three months. That's one-tenth the amount of carbon produced by a traditional burial.

There's some tension between the traditional cemetery industry and the green burial movement. The reaction to natural burial at one time was as bad as when funeral directors first confronted the growing popularity of cremation in the 1960s.

Often, cemeteries only begin to offer green burials in response to public pressure. They're seen as what one doesn't buy. Funeral directors may be tempted to discourage them simply because they reduce cash flow. In a study published in the journal Mortality, researchers attributed the slow acceptance of green burial at least in part to the profit-driven funeral industry, though family and religious considerations also play a role.

As green burial has become better known, advocates have been alarmed by an upsurge in "greenwashing," the making of false or misleading claims about environmental impacts, by the death care industry. Many suppliers offer services that only masquerade as green burials. People shopping for end-of-life services are warned of unverifiable claims and certifications that are financially tied to companies pushing supposedly green products.

The Federal Trade Commission in the U.S. has been urged to develop stricter standards for claims of eco-friendly funeral services and methods of disposition as part of its updated Green Guide.

The entertainment industry has played a role in popularizing the movement. Advocates credit HBO's *Six*

Feet Under with mainstreaming the concept. The series, which ran in the early 2000s, was widely regarded as one of its best, following the often-dysfunctional lives of a fictional family in the funeral business. The green burial of one principal character was portrayed as a deeply moving experience for his mourners. The episode did more to sell the idea of natural burial to the public than news stories. Reviews lauded its "compelling script" and the character of Nate Fisher, "the show's dazed, confused, but ultimately decent freethinker who's laid to rest six feet under – in the most natural of ways."

The Willow Casket Collective

Julie Stinson and Sian Turner are among five friends who've formed their own collective in Nova Scotia, producing an unusual kind of disposition container, wicker caskets, for what's likely to be a growing market.

Collective staff weave caskets by hand using hand-harvested willow rods.

The willow casket

The Willow Casket Collective is a small new operation in Antigonish County in the east-coast Canadian province, where most of the willow is grown. And now they're getting inquiries from across the country. The group weaves caskets, which are already popular in the United Kingdom, and has plans to make woven cremation urns. The willows are all hand-harvested, rod by rod.

Four women and one man are involved in the project, including a couple who are farmers and market gardeners and do the weaving during the off-season, Stinson explained. One customer with a terminal illness, who recently turned 80, "feels really good about making the decision to buy his casket while he's still alive," she said.

Chapter 7: Mycelium – Nature's True Recycler

"The cool thing is that mycelium has the ability to neutralize the toxins from the body and the soil and turn it into nutrients." – Bob Hendrikx, Founder of Loop Biotech.

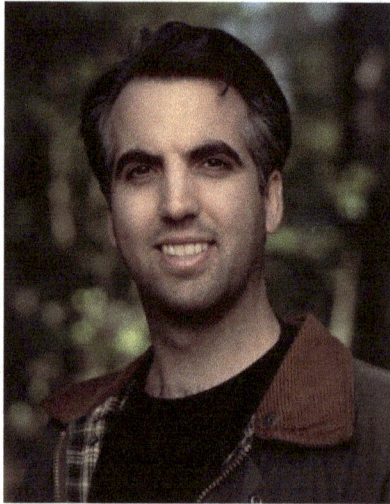

Bob Hendrikx,
founder of Loop Biotech

Mycelium coffins are not the first technology to be called a new normal in funerals. But, along with other new approaches to the disposition of human bodies in the greenest-possible ways, using mycelium or mushroom fiber is showing promising signs of literally taking root.

"That's definitely what we're aiming for. It's how nature does it," bio-designer and architect Bob Hendrikx said from his Loop Biotech company headquarters in Delft, the Netherlands.

"The way it's been done for too many years, preparing a person's body for disposition by cutting down a beautiful tree for a coffin, putting the body in a concrete box, and letting it rot for 10 or 20 years doesn't make a lot of sense."

Mycelium coffins are made from mushroom fiber, are 100 percent biodegradable, and promote the rapid decomposition of the body.

Hendrikx was a 25-year-old undergraduate in bio-design at Delft University of Technology when he first developed the concept of placing human bodies in a mushroom coffin, resting on a cushion of fungi. The first disposition of a human body using his rapidly composting "living coffin" took place in late 2020.

The coffin, which looks a bit like Styrofoam, is made from mycelium, a rootlike fungus structure found in soil and many other substances.

"Mycelium is nature's recycler," said Hendrikx. "While traditional methods pollute the soil, for us, it was a no-brainer, and the cool thing about it is that the process can actually be much cheaper than producing a wood coffin."

There is no wood or metal in the mushroom coffins themselves, though wood chips are added as food for the mycelium. They are regarded as suitable caskets for both traditional and natural burials.

Decomposition of a body using a traditional method, by casket burial or the green burial process, can take at least a decade, and much longer if a thick casket with varnished wood and metals is used. Mycelium grows in a matter of days, adding nutrients to the soil, Hendrikx explained. Trees, of course, take years to grow.

While still requiring burial space, the body meets the natural environment much faster than in a conventional coffin, and the mycelium and microorganisms within the moss accelerate the decomposition process. "Therefore, the body degrades faster," Hendrikx said.

The mycelium coffins disappear in less than two months, and the bodies are returned to the earth within three years. "Nature does all the work," Hendrikx explained.

He founded the start-up Loop Biotech and, as of 2022, the company had delivered living cocoons to six countries: the Netherlands, Belgium, Germany, Austria, the UK and the U.S. It's expanded its Netherlands-based production facility to 13,000 square feet (1,200 square meters) and was by late 2023 approaching production of 500 mycelium-based coffins a month. It employs over 100 and has had coverage from U.S. news networks, European magazines, and business media.

Hendrikx, who worked in his twenties as a research associate at MIT, obtained seed funding from two large Dutch funeral cooperatives and is focusing on getting large investments. Loop Biotech received the 2021 ASN Bank Award, a Dutch prize for sustainable start-ups that "make the world a little greener."

Benefits to the Soil

In 2023, the company launched three new designs. A Living Cocoon, a Forest Bed, and Loop Earthrise.

"The Living Cocoon is not only 100-percent biodegradable, it also enhances biodiversity," said the Funeral Service Times of the UK.

"It is grown in just seven days using a combination of mycelium and upcycled hemp fibers, and it can hold up to 200 kilograms (about 440 pounds) while itself weighing around 30 kilograms (about 66 pounds). Certified by the Funeral Furnishing Manufacturers' Association (FFMA), it is suitable for both traditional and natural burials, as well as cremation. Its rapid decomposition process ensures that the body contributes to the regeneration of the earth, rather than polluting it."

The company invites inquiries and orders from funeral directors everywhere through its website at loop-biotech.com. "Not only is his technology eco-friendly," Hendrikx said, "we actually have a positive environmental impact because what we do is recover the polluted soil that's in the ground from decades of wrong burial and chemicals in our bodies.

"The cool thing," he explained, "is that mycelium has the ability to neutralize the toxins from the body and the soil and turn it into nutrients that new plants can absorb and thereby increase biodiversity."

Following the 1986 nuclear plant disaster in Ukraine, mycelium was employed to start cleaning the soil. A lot of government industrial sites also clean their soil with mycelium, an organism that lives everywhere in the world, even in deserts.

"So, it's actually fortifying the soil instead of polluting it," Hendrikx said. "That's the biggest change we're making." Ninety-two percent of all plant species rely on mycelium to survive, he added. "It's the biggest recycler on earth."

Competitive Pricing

Loop Biotech's price per coffin, excluding shipping costs, is competitive with most other disposition methods, including cremation and alkaline hydrolysis. The mushroom coffins can be ordered online at a total price of €1,495 ($1,631USD/$2,079CAD), and with a discounted buy-now-pay-later voucher.

International attention has led to increased interest, particularly from Northern Europe, where there's more consciousness about the environment and understanding how the mushroom works as part of the ecosystem.

" The funeral industry is one of the most conservative and slow industries to adapt," Hendrikx said. But some companies have really proved they want to change. It helps that the mushroom coffins don't require huge investments in

71

new equipment or processes and can be accommodated within existing burial systems.

Frank Franse of the regional funeral organization, CUVO, said it's important for it to be involved in this kind of sustainable innovation: "It fits our objective to be a sustainable cooperative funeral service," he said.

Ed Bixby, founder of the Global Green Burial Alliance, is "impressed with the innovative concept" and is keen to learn more. "The cost," he said, "does seem most appropriate and not terribly expensive, but in comparison to conventional (methods), very affordable."

Anita van Loon, director of another service provider operating cemeteries in northern Holland, believes the product is coming along at an appropriate time as people look for a cleaner society and more natural funerals. "We give the body back to nature," she said. With young adults, "there will be a new generation interested in this new method. All the effort we've put into a cleaner way of living fits well with the natural way of dying."

The mycelium and raw materials all come from the Netherlands. "Most large coffin manufacturers in the Netherlands import their wood from Eastern Europe and call it sustainable," Hendrikx said. "Our vision is to enrich the world and save the natural world. That's the only reason we exist. The key is upscaling our facilities and production because we know people want it."

Loop Biotech has also formed a partnership with the Netherlands' largest natural burial organization, Nature Burials Netherlands. "The partnership," Hendrikx said, "allows customers to purchase a product and burial plot in advance, contributing to the restoration of natural environments."

Chapter 8: Human Body Composting – Next To Nature?

"Composting is what nature wants to do. It wants to create living things and then breaks those things down when they're no longer living." – Chandler Cummins, Advanced Composting Technologies

The objective of composting is to return the body to the earth by natural methods, just speeding it up.

Known more technically as Natural Organ Reduction, it's not unrelated to conventional burial, which, through natural processes, reduces a body to its most basic elements. It's just that composting takes considerably less time, as do other methods. The concept originated for use with livestock bodies.

Walt Patrick, stewardship manager at Herland Forest in Washington State, said that the community-based, not-for-profit cemetery was the state's first facility to offer natural organic reduction for human bodies and the first licensed operator for the procedure in the United States.

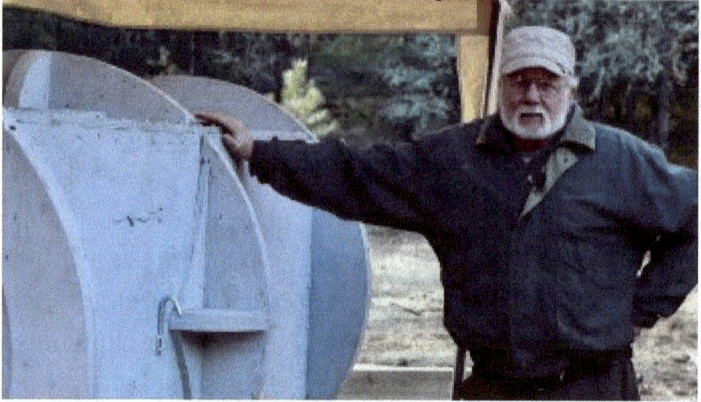

Walt Patrick of Herland Forest Natural Burial Cemetery in Washington has been developing an above-ground composting system called Natural Organic Reduction.

The cemetery uses similar methods to those of for-profit composting enterprises. The body is placed in a chamber and mixed with wood chips, moisture, and oxygen, plus added bacteria, protozoa, and fungi, turning it into compost within a matter of weeks. At Herland, the process operates off the power grid, using photovoltaic panels to supplement the heat in its chambers.

Herland also offers full-body burial, plus ash burial, ash scattering, and living-tree memorials. Its price for composting is $3,000, dropping to $2,700 if the family is directly involved. (The state requires a family member or an embalmer to lay the body to rest in an organic reduction cradle. The family's involvement saves the embalming fee.) At least three other companies are offering composting in Washington state, where the legislature approved the method in 2019.

Composting Slow to Gain State Approval

At the time of writing, human composting was legal in six states. Vermont, Colorado, and New York State legalized it in 2022, and in Oregon and Nevada in 2023 (which was to take effect in 2024). It was also legalized in California in 2022 (taking effect in 2027), over opposition from the state's Catholic Conference. Bills are also before several other state legislatures.

Composting human bodies is based on sound technology, says Chandler Cummins, development manager at Advanced Composting Technologies in North Carolina, who's worked in the field for over 15 years.

"It's just a different type of composting. It lets thermodynamics take over." Cummins said. "It's all about controls. You want to speed up what nature can do. The better the diet, the better the microbes are going to be, and you try to make them as happy as you can."

Katrina Spade, an architectural designer, founded her Seattle-based company, Recompose, in 2017. She said her company is part of the "death care revolution," in which bodies are placed in a reusable vessel with wood chips, alfalfa, and straw, combined with oxygen to increase microbial activity. Recompose bills itself as "a decidedly progressive outlook, drawing on queer feminist practices of inclusion and equity" and "committed to advocating and protecting the rights of BIPOC (black, indigenous and people of colour), religious minorities and undocumented people."

The composting 'pile,' as the New York Times described the process, will start "cooking. Bacteria release enzymes that break down tissue into component parts like amino acids and, eventually, the nitrogen-rich molecules bind with the carbon-rich ones, creating a soil-like substance." The heat kills common pathogens, the Times said. "Done correctly, there should be no smell."

The 131°F (55°C) heat generated by composting destroys most disease-causing pathogens. However, those who have died as a result of diseases such as Creutzfeldt-Jakob are not eligible for composting.

After about a month, the remains from composting are reduced to approximately one cubic yard (meter) of soil. These remains are given to the deceased person's family in the same manner as remains from cremation or to conservation groups that use them to rehabilitate forests.

Dr. Troy Hottle, senior analyst with Eastern Research and an early consultant on Spade's project, said that, opposed to ground burial and cremation, composting not only avoids the burden of carbon dioxide (CO_2), it advances the sequestering of carbon, reducing its release into the atmosphere. Less carbon in the atmosphere will reduce greenhouse gases and the impacts of climate change, he explained.

Recompose charges $7,000 for the disposition of a body, all costs included. The price covers transportation of the body from locations within Washington State. (A pre-payment plan can be arranged.) In 2023, Recompose was seeking crowdfunding to raise $5 million.

A third composting venture in Washington, Return Home, operates an 11,500-square-foot (1,070-square-meter) facility. Founder Micah Truman's trademarked 'Terramation' process transforms the body into soil by similar methods. His facility in Auburn, a Seattle suburb, charges $4,950 per body. Truman, whose background is finance, offers the natural organ reduction service directly to consumers in the U.S. and Canada and as a trade service, working with existing funeral homes, which will charge their own fees.

In Colorado, Seth Viddal, with coaching from Herland's Walt Patrick, has been providing composting vessels in a Denver warehouse. Viddal employs a 7x3-foot (2x9-meter) wooden box with wheels that allow it to be moved around, providing agitation and oxygen, helping the body achieve compost. He charges $7,900 per body, almost four times the cost of flame cremation.

Will It Sell?

Doubts, other than religious, have been raised about the viability and marketability of human composting.

Ed Bixby, former president of the California-based Green Burial Council, is skeptical about the demand for human composting. "I don't see a large market for this, at least not at this point in time," he said. "They're going to service people who want it, but, in my opinion, they're going to make a very small impact. I don't see people choosing this solution."

"The composting process isn't gentle," Bixby added, "contrary to how it's described. Organic reduction requires a lot of turbulence and moving parts that aren't so gentle. The gruesome details will be too much to bear for the grieving families. Quite honestly, it can be quite a brutal process. It's not like laying someone down on a bed of roses and having them disappear. I can't believe that you put grandma in a pile of mulch and a month later she's topsoil."

The relatively high cost is seen as a problem that may limit it to a niche market.

Death care consultant Shane Neufeld believes that, if the new method is ever going to hit the mainstream, it will require a lot of investment. However, he's skeptical that investors will invest unless there is evidence that the method is going to be popular enough to gain market share from cemeteries and cremation. "If I were speculating, I don't anticipate it's going to become terribly popular," he said.

Of the composting projects in Washington State, Bixby believes Herland Forest's concept is the best and most viable, albeit on a modest scale. "Walt Patrick at Herland," he said, "has been forthright and talked to the council about its work. He enlightened the council about the process, which up to that point was unclear."

Patrick had 30 years' experience composting large farm animals before he advanced into the disposition of human bodies. Herland Forest operates as a not-for-profit and has no investors to keep happy.

"We're not having to rush things in order to generate revenue to pay dividends to stockholders," Patrick said. "We're a non-profit with a paid-for facility. We don't feel we need to accelerate the process by grinding up the cadaver.

We're committed to allowing the process to proceed at its own pace."

As with both cremation and aquamation, Herland Forest will pulverize the bones after an extended period of decomposition. A camera goes into the chamber to inspect the remains so the body's state of decomposition won't be a matter of guesswork.

Bixby loves the "blue-sky" thinking, but worries companies like Recompose will be unable to produce enough revenue to service their debt and end up becoming a black eye for innovation in the funeral industry.

Hottle, formerly with the U.S. Environmental Protection Agency, has defended Recompose against media articles that disparage composting "as a grotesque way of treating bodies."

Some erroneously suggest the outcome will be made available commercially, with people spreading it on their lawns without realizing it. Instead, he said that composting provides a mechanism to dispose of a body respectfully, with no carbon footprint.

"The biomass of the body itself is retained in the soil," Hottle said. "The green burial folks will likely see it as sort of hand-in-hand to their approach as a low-energy way without necessitating land use."

Flame cremation has its distasteful aspects, as does the body's disintegration in a casket, he added.

"It's important," said Hottle, to understand how science copes with a growing population and the level of mortality that goes with it. He doesn't necessarily see composting as the sole answer to the coming crisis, with millions of deaths of baby boomers forecast over the next few decades.

"I don't know if there's any one answer," he said. "I don't think we can take all the options off the table. Creating more environmentally-friendly options will enable people to make choices in line with what they prefer to happen to their bodies. The more people there are, the more significant any impacts associated with deaths will be."

Human composting is still in its infancy and not widely available. Josh Slocum, former director of the Funeral Consumers Alliance, noting the Recompose $7,000 fee, suggested the price point has to change if it's ever going to be a viable option for most.

" Families who need to spend less are going to go for what's affordable, whatever the technology may be," he said. Options like human composting are generally only practical for people who "have the disposable income and inclination to do so" unless the companies' volumes can moderate their costs.

Chandler Cummins agrees that price is a problem but thinks scale might change that: "You can sell what the market can bear, and people want alternatives, but you can also overprice yourself and never get a sale. If they're only going to get a hundred or so people a year, they're going to have to charge one thing. If they're going to get 10,000 people, they can charge something else."

Chapter 9: The Outliers – Sea, Sky, Space, Mushrooms...

"I don't think we can take all the options off the table."
– Bioengineer Troy Hottle.

With mortality numbers growing and casket burials and flame cremation increasingly seen as distasteful, costly, and environmentally unfriendly, the search for alternative methods of human disposal continues.

Some new options are more practical than others, while some remain unproven and are likely dead ends. A number are extravagant and don't really offer alternatives.

Sea Burials

Most governments permit bodies to be disposed of at sea. It's a long-standing disposition option for ocean lovers. The body, suitably prepared and weighted, is dropped into the sea from a ship or plane. At present, few countries have policies in place that cover sea burials of cremated remains specifically.

Reef Burials

Memorial or eternal reefs involve artificially constructed marine habitats. The cremated bodies of people seeking green burial options can be laid to rest as a part of these artificial reefs, becoming a habitat for marine life.

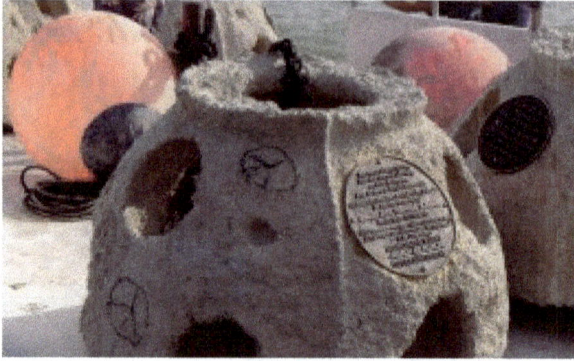

Memorial or eternal reefs are artificial marine habitats where the cremated remains of those seeking green burial options can be laid to rest.

In areas where coral reefs have been destroyed, artificial structures like reef balls have been used for years to repair damage. Memorial reef balls, made with the addition of remains from the dead, are a newer invention. Thousands of memorial reef balls with the cremated remains have already been sunk off the eastern seaboard of the United States and elsewhere.

A unique form of memorialization, reef balls will be of special interest to ocean lovers concerned with the marine environment.

Bodies in Orbit

SpaceX rockets launched cremated remains of 47 humans or a portion of them into orbit in 2022. It was the 18th time for such space 'burial' flight, costing upwards of $5,000 to fly one gram of "participant" remains into orbit.

Since 1994, Celesta has flown cremated remains on 15 different rockets into sub-orbital flights and six into Earth's orbit. Two NASA astronauts departed Earth this way, as did Star Trek actor James "Scotty" Doohan in 2008.

Sky Burial

Also called 'bird-scattered,' 'excarnation,' or 'celestial burial,' it is the funeral practice in which a human body is placed on a mountaintop or tower to decompose while exposed to the elements or eaten by scavenging animals, mainly carrion birds.

Buddhists teach transmigration and see no need to preserve the body, which is considered an empty vessel. But sky burial is a fading tradition, and few such places remain in operation today.

Mushroom Suit

In a variation on mycelium-based interment, artist Jae Rhim Lee developed an "infinity burial suit" involving flesh-eating mushrooms purportedly breaking down human bodies, cleansing them of toxins, and returning the remains to soil.

TV actor Luke Perry died of a stroke in 2019 at 52 and was buried in a mushroom suit. At last report, Coeio, her California company that specializes in green burial solutions, was still taking orders online for its Infinity Burial Suit.

Capsula Mundi

This, an organic egg-shaped pod (translated as 'world's capsule'), was designed by two Italian artists. They say the pods would contain a tree or seed, fertilized by a decomposing body in a fetal position, and planted in a forested area. The pod would allow a body to add to the soil's nutrients and become part of the natural landscape. So far, however, Capsula Mundi is marketing only biodegradable urns to be used for cremated ashes. The burial pod "is not yet ready for the market."

Promession

This technology, based on freeze-drying, was intended for the disposition of bodies in an eco-friendly way. Promession received extensive media attention in 2001. Invented by the late Swedish biologist Susanne Wiigh-Mäsak, it was in development stages for almost 20 years. Wiigh-Mäsak died in 2020, but her project, at last word, was still seeking investors.

Body Farms

They are legitimate research facilities where decomposition can be studied, particularly for forensic purposes. They were conceived in 1987 by anthropologist William Bass, an anatomical researcher and forensic anthropologist who began studying the processes and timetables involved in human body decay at the University of Tennessee.

Individuals agree to have their remains used for this purpose. Their bodies are placed outside in the elements to give researchers the opportunity to study natural decomposition.

The research conducted at these farms has done more than boost understanding of decomposition. There are applications in anthropology, forensic science, law enforcement, and related disciplines. Many investigators use body farms in criminal cases, as well as deaths by fire, drowning, or other causes.

Seven such facilities exist across the United States. Similar ones operate in Australia and Canada, the most recent in the province of Quebec.

Bass retired in his seventies but remained an active researcher. At 96, Bass made no apology for the work he has performed, although he said, "You've got to laugh to keep your sanity."

Chapter 10: Cemeteries – 'Forgotten Landscapes'

"Burial is dead. It's going to go away. It's not sustainable. Too many people and not enough land." –
Joseph Wilson, Bio-Response Solutions

'Landscapes of Death' are what two American academics referred to in a 2010 paper, drawing attention to the cemetery space shortage back then and the challenges facing traditional burial.

'Planning for the Disposal of the Dead' is the title of the paper by planning professors Carlton Basmajian and Christopher Coutts of universities in Iowa and Florida. "Cemeteries become a visual reminder of mortality," they wrote, pointing out that they produce increased traffic and noise as well. "On the other hand," they said, "Cemeteries also provide valuable open spaces and visual release, especially in dense urban neighborhoods."

Many urban cemeteries are running out of space to accommodate future burials (credit: John Rob).

The word 'cemetery' comes from the Greek, meaning 'sleeping places.' Cemeteries are seen as treasured sites for the memorialization of departed family members and friends, promising that the dead won't be forgotten. They're often lovely places to visit, whether or not you know people buried there. But with many running short of space, especially in larger urban centers, it's doubtful that they can accommodate the vast numbers of bodies coming their way.

In their research paper, Basmajian and Coutts looked at baby-boom demographics at the end of the century's first decade, projecting what was likely to come in the next few years. "There are 78 million boomers in the United States alone," Basmajian said in the 2010 report. "You're talking about 3.5 to 3.7 million deaths a year in the United States, about a million more than we're facing right now."

If all these bodies were buried in standard burial plots, the authors estimated, that would eat up 130 square miles (337 square kilometers) of pure grave space, not counting roads, trees, or pathways. But there have been no major cemeteries built in the United States since about 1950.

Many attribute the problem of diminishing cemetery space to a lack of foresight on the part of cemetery operators, governments, particularly local ones, and the planning profession itself. All failed to anticipate or at least plan for the enormous number of deaths on the horizon.

Worldwide deaths are projected to increase from 62 million in 2024 to between 68 million in 2030, then forecast to reach 114 million in 2075 and 123 million in 2100. As Prof. Basmajian says, we as a society have no sense of what's coming.

Limitations on Land Use

There are an estimated 145,000 cemeteries or graveyards in the United States, covering about a million acres (405,000 hectares), plus 18,000 known ones in Canada and 14,000 in the United Kingdom. Many are now closed to new burials, though open for the interment of ashes.

The United States may actually face a shortage of space for cemeteries, mainly in urban areas. Countries such as England and others in Europe have already run out of usable land and are now exhuming graveyards, burying coffins on top of each other, and even digging up old sites to cremate the remains.

A 2013 survey showed half of the cemeteries in the United Kingdom, with a population of over 67 million and a land mass of 94,058 square miles (243,610 square kilometers), won't have room for new burials by the 2030s.

Despite its land mass of almost 3,088,815 square miles (8 million square kilometers), Australia, with 27 million people, has the same problem with cemeteries reaching overload. Many are expected to exhaust their space within 30 years; in New South Wales, within 10 years. Roughly 170,000 Australians die each year, and close to a third are buried in cemeteries.

Challenges for Future Land Use

"Planning for new cemeteries is fraught with challenges," Coutts and Basmajian pointed out, while also noting that "cemeteries are not necessarily perceived to make good neighbors."

Land for cemetery use is allocated permanently, they noted, which makes long-range land-use planning critical. But there's little contemporary guidance for planners on how to project the land-use needs of the deceased, given the increased popularity of cremation, but also non-traditional burial methods becoming more available.

Erik Lees, a land-use planner who's designed cemeteries across the United States and Canada, calls them 'the forgotten landscapes.' "The planning profession," he said, "hasn't had cemeteries on its radar, at least until recently. I have to ask my friends in the profession, 'who's been asleep at the switch for the last 30 years?' while they've dealt with employment lands, agricultural lands, housing, transportation, and all those other land-use issues," Lees said. "You have to build hospitals and build schools and parks, but you've also got to build cemeteries."

Basmajian agrees that the planning and development world hasn't talked enough about the cemetery space problem. "Big cities like New York and San Francisco face some real constraints because of the cost of development and the price of land," he said. "In Sydney, Toronto, Boston, and London, it's not so much that they're running out of space as much as they're not really planning for what the long-term management of those spaces will be."

"At the local level, governments need to be thinking about how to maintain lands over time," Basmajian said, recommending that "states should be setting policy to encourage local governments to consider this in their financial planning models."

Who Owns a Burial Plot?

Laws governing burial plots in cemeteries vary widely. Most cemeteries don't sell plots of land; they sell interment rights. These rights are like leases, called renewable lots. The purchaser doesn't own the ground but has the exclusive right to be buried in the plot. Owners have the right to determine the manner of burial, complying with the deceased person's wishes. Some allow a burial rights owner to pre-authorize or pre-arrange their own manner of interment.

The rights are not owned by the deceased person, who can't own rights or property, but are normally held by family members. These can be renewed and passed on from generation to generation, though they usually can't be sold or transferred without the cemetery's written permission. That allows the owner to keep the body of the deceased interred in the space virtually in perpetuity.

In many locations, the interment right is granted for 75 or 99 years. After several years, there's little left but bones and teeth, but it may take 50 years before a skeleton becomes brittle and crumbles, even longer in non-acidic soil. Often, when the exclusive right ends, the ground is reused by the cemetery, the remaining bones are removed and can be placed in an ossuary, or the grave is dug deeper to permit a new burial. Some cemeteries have sold rights or leases with no expiration date.

"We're going to have to look at high density in cemeteries," said Erik Lees. That would entail reusing family burial plots after a generation or so. "After 20 years, there's really nothing left through the magic of microbiology," he said.

In Australia, most leases are for an indefinite period, but some areas offer the option of leasing a grave for a limited period. Reusing grave sites has been legal in South Australia since the 1800s. Headstones are removed and crushed while the plot is recycled and reused.

A more extreme version of cemetery densification can be found in Vienna, with 1.9 million inhabitants and 550,000 graves in 46 cemeteries.

The University of Vienna's Erich Striessnig said that the graves have 10-year contracts, after which they're reused. "It might well be that this time will have to be shortened in the future," he added. It depends on how long it takes for a human body to decay sufficiently.

Standing Burial

Another option is the standing burial, placing the body upright in the grave rather than laying it to rest. This saves both money and space.

Bodies are buried vertically in this natural cemetery in Melbourne, Australia.

Kurweeton Road Cemetery, described as "a peaceful, pastoral setting" 124 miles (200 kilometers) west of Melbourne, Australia, is purposely left in a natural state. The 10-acre (4-hectare) cemetery, the first of its kind, is designed for standing burial exclusively. It has a capacity for 30,000 eco-friendly burials in plots a third the size of conventional graves. Bodies are first frozen (rather than embalmed), then placed in a biodegradable shroud and interred in a plot two feet square by ten feet deep (.6x.6x3 meters). The burial spaces are dug with an auger like those commonly used for utility poles. For every person buried there, a tree is planted on a nearby hill.

A related proposal in Australia would create a "burial belt" outside the country's urban areas, with green space, trees, and even the planting of vegetables. It would require natural burial, protecting wildlife and vegetation, with no embalming or headstones.

High-Rise Cemeteries

Some countries are finding other solutions, such as vertical cemeteries.

For example, in Asia, bodies may be buried in high-rise pagodas, including a 20-storey one in Taiwan, where photos and urns containing a deceased's ashes are kept behind a small window. It has the capacity to hold the ashes of 400,000 people. A 32-storey vertical cemetery, built in 1983 in Santos, Brazil, has space for 25,000 bodies. A Christian cemetery in Tughlakabad, India, built Asia's largest vertical cemetery with 300 crypts.

Not all are success stories. In Naples, Italy, in October 2022, the collapse of a second multi-storey marble coffin niche structure at a cemetery raised questions about the construction and maintenance of the structures. Coffins containing human remains were left hanging in the air after the collapse of the building called 'The Resurrection.' Fortunately, no one was hurt. Earlier that year, another marble structure in the same cemetery collapsed, destroying 300 burial niches.

Vertical cemeteries are an option in many countries, but the collapse of one in Naples, Italy, in 2022 raised concerns about construction standards.

However, there is opposition to high-rise burials, particularly in Europe. Verona, Italy, proposed a 330-foot-high (100-meter) futuristic tower cemetery but ran into opposition from citizens and politicians.

Future Cemeteries

In 2040, the 'decade of departure,' new cemeteries may be nothing like what we're accustomed to seeing. Dr. Karla Rothstein at Columbia University's School of Architecture is the founder of the DeathLab project, focused on reconceiving how people live with death. Its scholars and designers are developing two projects.

Perpetual Constellation uses sustainable technology for the disposition and memorialization of the dead, relying on an airless conversion of bodies to break down their organic matter and generate biogas, which can be used as fuel. With a capacity of 5,400 interments a year, it would accommodate about 10 percent of all annual deaths in a typical year in New York City.

Sylvan Constellation aims to increase the capacity of the Arnos Vale Cemetery in Bristol, England, within six years by using technology to double the capacity of earth burial. "Restored in 2003, Arnos Vale remains an active burial ground, also serving as a nature conservatory," said John Troyer, director of the Centre for Death & Society. Technology may mean that, in the future, the deceased can be memorialized in different ways. Future burial sites may feature QR codes or barcode squares. Visitors would scan the code to see pictures of or read about the deceased.

"There's a myth that people repeat that it's taboo to discuss death," he said. "The exact opposite is true. We humans discuss death and dying all the time. What we don't discuss is our own personal death. We all know that death is in the future.

"The reason we are still here as a species," Troyer said, "is because our ancestors were able to adapt to change."

Chapter 11: End-of-Life Stresses and Responsibilities

"Funerals are expensive, broken and exploitive. They have to change." – Nicole Archer, Social Media Producer, CNET

Don't put off planning till tomorrow.

" We've been shouting this for 30 years," said Sara Williams, president of the Funeral Consumers Alliance (FCA) in the United States. "Get your stuff together. You're going to die…it's not if, it's when. And if you wait till the last minute, it will be a hot mess."

The FCA's mission states that it's "dedicated to protecting a consumer's right to choose a meaningful, dignified, affordable funeral."

It supports informed consumer choice, assisting people to find information that helps them make decisions they can afford through its local affiliates throughout the country and by answering phone calls and emails in real time.

Sara Williams, President of the Funeral Consumers Alliance (FCA) in the United States

The issue needs to be "framed within the larger context, moving from a single consumer decision to the cultural setting in which funerary decisions are made," Williams said, adding that "consumers do not make decisions in a vacuum. They're influenced by their cultural milieu and what is considered customary."

"It's also an issue of 'intersectionality,'" she said, "depending on one's position in a local community, geographically and socially. Some individuals and groups, particularly those who are financially fragile, will have less or no ready access to lower-cost alternatives."

The FCA partnered with the Consumer Federation of America on research showing that most state funeral regulators offer little or no information to consumers about their rights, including how to file complaints, access disciplinary records, or compare funeral services. The alliance is also working with the Federal Trade Commission to update the 1984 Funeral Rule to require funeral homes to post prices online.

The FCA's emphasis on funeral education is key to developing beneficial relationships between the funeral industry and the consumer.

The education of consumers related to funerary matters has been and will continue to be an ongoing process. Williams recommended beginning this training at the high school level, since every year, more and more people are born who have not heard the message about planning ahead.

But there's also a place for newer voices, offering education and contemporary examples of meaningful after-death care and memorialization that don't exploit individuals or exacerbate poverty.

"There is much hope here and a call to action," Williams said. "Our work is never done."

Where to Start

Much of the difficulty involved in funerals can be mitigated through advance care planning.

Serious illness or an accident can easily leave anyone incapacitated and unable to make decisions. An advance directive, living will, or power of attorney articulates and documents one's wishes regarding medical treatment. Such a document ensures one's wishes are followed by healthcare providers and family. It often states preferences about when to withhold or withdraw life-sustaining treatment, whether or not one wants artificially provided nutrition or hydration when close to death or unconscious, and do-not-resuscitate (DNR) orders.

An executor, personal representative or administrator of the estate must determine the person's wishes regarding a funeral and disposition, obtain copies of the death certificate, determine if there is a last will, decide if probate or administration of the estate is needed and decide whether temporary administration of the estate is immediately required.

The directive may also include information about what procedures one requires upon death and general statements about end-of-life care, preferences for body disposition, organ or full-body donation, and any plans for memorials or services.

Reporting a Death

Once a doctor or nurse practitioner has made the death pronouncement, proper procedures must be followed. Registering a death requires two documents. The Medical Certificate of Death is a document completed by a medical professional (physician, coroner, or other authority) that details the cause of death and other medical information. The Statement of Death is a form filled out by a funeral director and an informant (usually a family member) containing personal information about the deceased, such as name, date of birth, and place of death. Both need to be filed with the appropriate government registration office.

Certified copies of the filed death certificate are needed to conduct several tasks. For example, one is required to allow transport of the body to the funeral home, burial location, crematory, or other location. The body may be taken directly to a family home from a hospital or residential care facility, but the transfer must be authorized by the executor or next of kin.

Families may ask funeral homes to hold a body temporarily for a short time as they make plans. "There's nothing wrong with a funeral home saying they'll hold your relative for two to three days for $250 in a temperature-controlled environment," death care advocate Shane Neufeld said. "And there's nothing wrong with a competing funeral home coming by to pick up the body. It happens all the time."

Shane Neufeld of Integrity Death Care

Some jurisdictions require a funeral director to file the death certificate, receive a body from a hospital, sign transfer permits, and oversee disposition. Others require a funeral director's involvement only when the deceased had a contagious disease. Municipalities and individual cemeteries, crematories, and other disposition facilities may or may not have their own requirements.

Following transfer, the body is generally washed, dressed, and cooled. It's necessary to protect those handling the body from exposure to health risks, known or unknown. If the person died from a contagious disease, the family must consult a doctor. Even if a hospital or care facility is pressing for a decision on the next steps, urgency is not necessary.

A timeline should be established to obtain all permits and authorizations, notify family and friends, allow for any cultural or religious observances, and prepare for the preferred disposition method. The deceased may have provided instructions before death about how a funeral will be handled. But the family has the right to make final decisions.

People should ask a lot of questions of prospective suppliers, either when buying services at the time of need or in advance, Neufeld urged. Don't buy from someone who doesn't advertise their price list fairly and accurately, he cautioned. And be careful of package discounts. "If I see a discount on a funeral home website, that's everything I need to know," he said. "That's an indicator of what you're dealing with."

Finally, Neufeld recommended, challenge the necessity of each itemized good or service, and never be afraid to ask a funeral home what its markup is. "If they feel uncomfortable telling you, that's a problem."

"Making arrangements in advance of a death doesn't mean you have to pre-pay," he said, "but you should have your ducks in a row. Make sure you're comfortable with who you're dealing with."

And there's nothing wrong with making the necessary arrangements and notifying friends and family of the pending death of a loved one.

"People sometimes feel funny about that," Neufeld said. "They feel like they're doing something disrespectful. But that's probably the best thing for themselves and the family. Don't feel odd or bad if you know the end is near."

The time for filing a death certificate varies, but it must be completed before other permits are issued and before final disposition. Be warned. Many copies of the death certificate may be needed. Survivors need to assemble any necessary documents and information to conclude the deceased's affairs.

These include:

- A last will
- Insurance policies
- Unpaid bills or debts
- Bank account numbers
- Online or credit card access codes or numbers
- Driver's license, vehicle ownership papers
- Government social or old-age security plans

- Income tax contacts
- Deeds to property
- Pension and other financial information
- Healthcare and public health cards.

Home Funerals

While we are most familiar with funerals conducted at a funeral home with guidance from professional staff, home funerals are an increasingly popular alternative and can be carried out legally and safely in most jurisdictions.

Often, intimate, loving, and affordable home-based death care allows family and friends to provide care to the deceased with minimal assistance. Families have the right to provide their own after-death care, but they're required to make arrangements with a local municipality, usually where the death occurred. As with conventional funerals, proper procedures must be followed, including necessary paperwork and time frames.

The body can be brought directly to a family home from a hospital or residential care facility, but the transfer must be authorized by the executor or next-of-kin. If the death occurs at home, the relatives must contact local emergency officials to take the deceased to a facility where a legal declaration of death can be made.

Family and friends must be notified, accommodations made for cultural or religious observances, and preparations made for the preferred method of disposition.

If family members wish to perform these duties, preparation of the body includes washing and dressing it, as well as providing a casket or shroud. Cooling will have to take place within eight hours of death, maintaining the body at 5°C (41°F), if necessary, by placing a cooling plate or blanket, ice packs, dry ice, or other cooling products around vital organs. People must be prepared for rigor mortis after death.

They also needn't be alarmed by an irregular pattern of breathing of someone on the brink of death, known as Cheyne Stokes (also sometimes called 'chain stokes'). The pattern may involve fast, shallow breathing followed by slow, heavier breathing and moments without any breath at all, called apneas.

Arranging for the care of a deceased family member is not always an easy task, but resources are available. The U.S.-based National Home Funeral Association was founded to educate and support individuals, families, and communities in death care. Created in 2010, its members come from all 50 states, five Canadian provinces, and seven other countries. With its all-volunteer board, the alliance is a resource for those contemplating or planning a home funeral.

Its website (www.homefuneralalliance.org) stresses that community death care is for everyone and strives to be open and receptive to all the ways home funerals can look and feel. A family may retain the services of clergy or a home funeral death doula who's trained to know the law, help find resources, and provide other services. The alliance discourages notions that one has to be anti-funeral director or anti-embalming to support home funerals. It welcomes people under the home funeral umbrella, including those who work in the funeral industry.

One of its goals is to ensure that educational materials are as accessible as possible, and it is constantly learning how it can improve services and welcomes feedback.

Environmental Concerns

Regardless of whether a funeral is conducted through a funeral director, through a co-operative, or at home, many of the same environmental concerns are relevant. Two of the least eco-friendly activities associated with funerals are driving long distances to attend and the purchase of flowers, particularly imported ones. It goes without saying that travelling to attend memorials can come with an environmental cost, depending on the distance.

Families may appreciate other sensible ways of receiving condolences. Many funeral homes have installed technology for remote viewing or live streaming of services. Sending flowers to grieving families is a traditional gesture. But flowers for funeral and memorial services have been called a beautiful waste. They don't last. And importing flowers from countries like Colombia makes little environmental sense.

Some flowers and arrangements can be chosen with fewer negative consequences. The florist can provide certification that flowers or potted plants were produced responsibly. Pesticide-free, organic flowers can be purchased from local growers or ordered online.

The closer the provider, the better. A frequently-used alternative to flowers is a financial donation, usually to the deceased's preferred charity.

The eco-minded might also ask for plants or trees.

Living Funerals

A living funeral is a unique celebration of life. Memorial services are normally held after a person's death, but a recent trend is to hold one for someone who's aware they're living in their final days. Planning your own funeral is not an easy subject for some, especially for those who've been given a terminal prognosis.

For a person living with a terminal diagnosis, other people's feelings can be difficult. But it can also be important to the person's psychological state and that of the dying person's family to attend the living funeral. It is sometimes used as a time to read the will and explain the reasons behind some of the decisions contained within it. It's often just an opportunity to spend time together, exchange memories, and a final goodbye, and bring comfort to everyone.

Those who've been guests at a living funeral say it can be an invaluable experience to feel an outpouring of love from family and friends and show appreciation for what they've given over the years.

Job Stress for Funeral Home Staff

If planning one funeral is stressful for a family, imagine the stress that funeral directors and those who work for them have. They're generally on call 24/7, performing a valuable, often stressful, and not always appreciated service. Those in the field have knowledge that can help and support families when they need it most.

They labour tirelessly to keep up with demand. In the last century, the funeral business has become a mammoth industry. Its growth has not always been for the best of reasons or with the best of intentions, or with the best results for families.

That's not a reflection on all funeral directors or funeral homes. As in any line of business, there are good and bad, and it is a business, one that many of us will rely on when the time comes. At least one study has shown that stress and depression are common among funeral directors and those who work for them.

A 2019 Harvard University research study by sociologist Jessica McClanahan focused on the trauma that mortuary workers are directly exposed to through body handling and preparation. "They may also face additional work stressors in their dealings with the bereaved," she wrote. "Through bereavement and counselling, mortuary workers may also be exposed to aversive details of trauma to the deceased or become fatigued by the emotional weight of their counselling duties."

There's reason to believe that many of these individuals meet clinical criteria for trauma exposure, McClanahan wrote. Civilian mortuary workers are not exposed to traumatic death as frequently or severely as those in military or disaster situations.

But their exposure is ongoing throughout their careers and includes those who have come to unnatural ends such as homicide, suicide, auto accidents, drownings and fires. Interacting with the families of these victims adds to the trauma.

Historically, working with the dead was assigned to lower social classes. While this may no longer be the case, the stigma still lingers and "morticians and funeral directors are painfully aware of the common negative stereotype of people in their occupations," she wrote.

Funeral Director Caleb Wilde is known for his award-winning book *Confessions of a Funeral Director: How Death Saved My Life*, his blog of the same title, and his appearances on YouTube. Wilde refers to his blog as "irreverent, yes, insensitive, no." His second book, All the Ways Our Dead Still Speak, deals with a funeral director's perspectives on life, death, and the hereafter.

Funeral director and author Caleb Wilde

Wilde can be an outspoken critic of his industry. "Not only is it unfriendly to the environment, it's also unfriendly to the way we approach death," he said in a TEDx Talk. "The professionalism of death care has brought us some wonderful things. But there are sustainable options that are environmentally friendly and death-embracing."

Wilde's writing doesn't mask the fact that he struggles constantly with depression, burnout, and stress. Being faced almost daily with death, especially the death of children, has been extremely difficult for him.

He attributes much of the mental burden borne by funeral service workers to bosses and co-workers who don't understand stress management techniques. At his funeral home, he tries to create a working environment where employees can share their needs and emotions.

Chapter 12: Funeral Poverty – The Crisis Already Here

"Death of a cherished loved one may be emotionally devastating for the living, but it also may be economically shattering." – Victoria Haneman, Creighton University School of Law

It's an old complaint. Prices are rising and everything costs too much, from eggs to housing to funerals.

The costs of dying are too often deferred by family members until the last minute as they deal with what they see as more pressing needs. Many of us are unable or unwilling to plan for our own deaths, leaving family members to cope with the costs and arrangements when the need actually arises.

For families living near or below the poverty line, the loss of a loved one can be financially devastating. However, there is hope in several affordable and eco-friendly options that are becoming increasingly available. But the earlier they make these choices, the better.

Funeral poverty has become a crisis at the very time that literally billions are expected to reach the ends of their lives in the next four or five decades. Unfortunately, too many of us are uninformed, unprepared, negligent or simply too gullible to make the best choices for our pocketbooks and the environment.

Victoria Haneman, a law professor at Creighton University, writes extensively about the death care industry (credit: SevenPonds).

"Families face potentially devastating death care costs when they're called on to make sudden choices at the demise of parents, siblings, or other relatives, and even, tragically, for children. Failure to provide for oneself or one's dependents," Victoria Haneman, a former professor at the Creighton School of Law in Nebraska, wrote, "is stigmatized and often accompanied by feelings of shame, inadequacy, and inferiority."

"Bereavement compounds this sense of failure when not being able to pay for the ritualization and memorialization that reflect societal and cultural beliefs," she said. "These values translate to dishonoring or disrespecting the dead." But the death of a loved one "is not viewed as the appropriate time to bargain shop for cheap alternatives."

In that sense, funerals are not for the dead, but for the living.

Over 100 years ago, care of the deceased was mostly done at home or in a religious setting. In the 20th century, the idea of an outsider 'serving' a family during this time came to be seen as a status marker that one could afford this service.

"Now," said Sara Williams, President of the Funeral Consumers Alliance in the United States. "The funeral industry has grown into a multi-billion-dollar enterprise, with effective lobbying at the state and federal levels. The industry is instrumental in perpetuating the idea that the type of funeral one selects for a deceased loved one and what items are part of that ceremony are signs of one's esteem for that person," Williams said.

Funeral Poverty is Widespread

Lower-income families in the U.S. spend far more on death care services relative to household expenditures than high-income families, Haneman wrote. Expensive goods such as watches and boats are status items for the wealthy; the funeral is a notable expenditure among lower-income families in the United States.

In 2014, the top one percent spent less on funerals than everyone else as a share of total spending. "Conversely, the poor spend a 26-percent greater share of total expenditures than the national average (on funerals)," she noted.

More and more families are living below the poverty line in all countries, including the wealthiest, than ever before. The poverty line is generally defined as 50 percent of the median household income.

A low-income family of four in the United States brings in about $25,000 a year; in Canada, about $26,000 (CAD).

Eighteen percent of UK families live below the poverty line. One survey found that most Americans have merely $1,000 in savings, which severely limits options in the event of an unexpected death in the family.

The U.S. poverty rate increased to 12.4 percent in 2022 from 7.8 percent a year earlier. "By far, this is the largest annual increase in U.S. history for both children and the overall population in terms of poverty, going back to 1967," said one report from Columbia University. A 2023 survey showed that more than 61 percent of Americans were living paycheck to paycheck.

A fall 2023 poll showed nearly half of Canadians living from payday to payday as costs of living and dying continue to rise. Statistics Canada in 2023 projected poverty at 10.2 percent, a significant increase from the official poverty rate in 2021 of 7.4 percent or 2.7 million people, including 1.7 percent in deep poverty.

In Australia, more than 3.32 million people, or 13.4 percent of the 26.7 million population, live below the poverty line.

By 2023, 15 million people in the United Kingdom lived below the poverty line, 2.1 million of them pensioners.

A report on funeral poverty in the United Kingdom was released by SunLife in early 2025. The 21st annual Cost of Dying report said 100,000 grieving families in the United Kingdom were having financial difficulty covering funeral bills. The cost of a simple, attended funeral had risen 3.5 percent in a year to £4,285, while unattended cremations had risen 6.7 percent to £1,597, the report said.

While two-thirds of people make provisions to pay for their own funeral, only 38 percent leave enough to cover the whole cost. This lack of provision means that, on average, families are left to cover a shortfall of £1,695. That totals almost £1 billion across the UK.

For one in five bereaved families, around 100,000, covering this cost causes 'notable financial concerns' and a total unpaid funeral debt of £240,000,000. While it is sometimes possible to release money from the deceased's bank accounts for funeral costs before probate has taken place, a third of families are still left to cover at least some of the costs themselves, with 10 percent taking on debt to do so. In some cases, loved ones were asked for money and even to sell their belongings to cover the costs.

Seventy-five percent said paying for a funeral impacted their mental health, while 60 percent said it impacted their physical health, according to the SunLife report.

The report found that 33 percent of people who had recently organized a funeral said the cost-of-living crisis impacted how they organized and paid for it. One in five said paying for the funeral impacted their own standard of living. Eight percent had to cut back on essential items, and six percent had struggled to pay essential bills.

A study for the U.S. National Institutes of Health on the impact of poverty and deprivation at the end of life found that people in economically resource-rich countries who are in poverty are likely to die younger with increased co-morbidities.

More than 183,000 Americans died in 2019 because of poverty, making it the fourth greatest cause of death, according to a report published by the Journal of the American Medical Association in 2023. That was 10 times the number of homicides that year, it said.

In England and Wales, nearly 30,000 excess winter deaths were attributed to cold weather and high energy costs.

"Millions of U.S. households are considered low income, but earning just over the poverty threshold," wrote Sara Marsden-Ill in 2020 for US.funerals.com. "This means that a huge number of Americans fall into the quite staggering bracket of low-income or poverty. So, almost half of the nation could be classified as in dire financial circumstances," she said.

"With so many families on low income and struggling to make ends meet month to month, it comes as no surprise that we are entering an era of what is being termed funeral poverty," Marsden-Ill said.

She cited one funeral director recalling 40 years earlier, when people were more aware of their own mortality and had insurance or put money aside. "They understood that they were going to die. I don't know if we are wrapped up in immortality, but people don't think about it now," she wrote.

How Much Does a Burial Cost?

The National Funeral Directors Association in 2023 estimated the median cost of a funeral and burial in America at around $9,420, not including a burial plot or flowers, and transportation. However, the cost can range as high as $15,000 to $20,000 or more, depending on the family's wishes, wealth, and the cost of burial plots. Since the pandemic, the cost of dying has radically increased.

A study ranked Hawaii as the most expensive state to hold a funeral. Researchers said the high price of land in the state is a 'massive contributor' to its funeral costs. California came in as the second most expensive place to hold a funeral, with ceremonies costing $10,727 on average. It was followed by Oregon, New York, and Massachusetts, where funerals also cost over $10,000 on average.

Between 2011 and 2019, average funeral costs in the United Kingdom grew 42 percent from £2,971 to £4,202, increasing to more than £9,000 when professional fees and discretionary extras such as memorials, flowers, and catering costs were included. The local council or hospital can arrange a Public Health Funeral if there isn't enough money in the estate to pay for it and if there are no relatives or friends available to arrange the funeral. The local council decides the time and date, but extras like flowers, cars, or newspaper notices aren't included.

In Australia, an average funeral can cost $2,000 and up.

How Much Does Cremation Cost?

Flame cremation with a service can be a bargain compared to casket burial, with an average cost of just under $7,500 in the United States. In this case, the service involves most of the same costs and procedures associated with burial, minus the casket.

The American Association of Retired Persons says the cost of basic cremation can be as low as $700, while the Cremation Research Council says the average cost of a direct cremation is $1,100 and that 41 percent of consumers opt for that choice.

In New Zealand, basic cremation costs as little as $525 to $900.

For flame cremation itself, federal laws don't dictate container requirements, but certain states and provinces may require an opaque or non-transparent container, a corrugated cardboard box, or a wooden casket. Many casket manufacturers provide caskets specially built for cremation. For most direct cremations, there's no need to buy a casket at all. A less-expensive heavy cardboard box, referred to as an 'alternative container,' is sufficient.

Why Does It Cost So Much?

"Death has become a large, lucrative, bureaucratic corporate business over five generations," Prof. Haneman told this writer. "The business of death is being managed by 'a death care industrial complex' with 2023 revenues estimated at $68 billion in the United States alone," she said.

"I'm writing about the economics of death care and how to reduce costs for consumers. It's the traditional open-casket method of disposition that's driving prices up. The consumer is generally inexpert and vulnerable at the time of bereavement," Haneman said, noting that decisions are too often time-pressured and perceived as irreversibly final.

As a result, the industry has benefited from consumer uncertainty. She cites, "Shareholder reports that reveal that the largest corporate providers, including Dignity in the UK and Service Corporation International in the U.S., all explicitly rely on their pre-need markets as an in-house growth solution to keep their shareholders happy and to inspire confidence in prospective investors."

In its March 2023 Investor Factsheet, SCI boasted of being "poised to benefit from aging of America, using U.S. Census Bureau data to divide the population into three categories of potential consumers, organized by age group: 'pre-need' cemetery customer: age 55-64, 'pre-need' funeral customer: age 65-74 and 'at-need' customer: age 75 plus.

"By treating every citizen as a potential sale," Haneman said, "such modelling ambitiously, if somewhat misleadingly, imagines absolute market capture. Everybody will die, so every living American is a prospective SCI customer…at least for the purpose of attracting investors."

The corporations tout their 'premier pre-need sales program' as a key investment consideration and significant market opportunity. They promise investors to deliver ongoing and reliable growth and shareholder returns via, among other things, "annual pre-need sales of more than $2 billion and a $14-billion backlog of future revenues from pre-need sales.

All funeral directors providing funerals financed through pre-need arrangements are participating in the delivery of a 'pre-need product,' but there are seismic differences in the way and extent to which funeral companies market pre-need products to consumers and investors.

Billion-Dollar Industry

A major contributing factor in the cost of funerals is the consolidation of funeral homes into the hands of a few corporate giants and private equity firms. The Funeral

Consumers Alliance and the Consumer Federation of America reported in 2017 that corporations like Service Corporation International (SCI) charge median prices for their death care product 47 to 72 percent higher than at other funeral homes. The 2017 median price of a simple cremation: $1,562 at independent funeral homes, but $2,700 at SCI facilities. Their investors didn't seem to mind, as stocks rose 151 percent over five years, they said.

"The multibillion-dollar funeral industry, a universal service that everyone has to deal with at some point, has hiked costs to the consumer by 4.7 percent, a rate well above last year's overall inflation rate of 3.4 percent," Luke Goldstein reported in the January 2024 American Prospect Magazine.

He cited the example of a cemetery in Maryland that jacked up prices after it was bought by Dignity LLC, owned in turn by SCI. After the purchase, the cemetery began hiking the final prices for all its burial rights holders. He called SCI "the largest monopolistic actor that's wrapped its tentacles around death care nationwide."

"One of the reasons funeral homes, in particular, get away with price-gouging," Goldstein said, "is that the industry doesn't operate like other goods where consumers can just wait until market fluctuations bring costs down."

" Without serious systemic change, there will be no end to the vulgarity in profiteering from death that people now recognize acutely," predict William McGowan and Samantha Fletcher, two UK academics who have studied the issue extensively. They've long emphasized that the rising cost of death care is becoming a huge burden for lower- and middle-class families. Their analysis of the UK industry, however, suggests a sea change is unlikely under current regulatory frameworks.

Inability to pay these rising costs," Fletcher said, "means the growth of personal debt and funeral poverty."

Questionable Pricing Policies

The failure of many funeral homes to be transparent about prices is contributing to the expenses for families.

For example, in 2023, personnel with the Federal Trade Commission (FTC) placed undercover calls across the U.S. to more than 250 funeral providers asking for price information. In January 2024, the FTC issued a stern warning to 39 funeral homes for failing to reveal their general price lists to callers by phone. Staff found that these providers violated the FTC's regulations under its Funeral Rule, intended to regulate the industry.

Those companies received warning letters emphasizing their obligations under the Funeral Rule, stating they should take prompt remedial action and reminding them that noncompliance may result in penalties of up to $51,744 per violation.

The fundamental compliance principle is that, if a consumer calls with price questions, the funeral home must respond on the phone. They can't require consumers to come to the funeral home in person to get price information.

On one call, a funeral home said the local health code required the body to be embalmed, although most states do not require it or only under certain circumstances. Yet another funeral home promised to send a general price list but instead sent a list of package prices, contrary to Funeral Rule requirements.

Among the most common complaints of U.S. consumers, as in the UK, is the failure of most funeral homes to list their General Price Lists (GPLs) online, which they say should be required under the Funeral Rule. By June of 2022, only 16-18 percent of U.S. funeral homes had posted price lists online.

There had been calls for the commission to modernize the Funeral Rule to require all funeral providers who maintain an online presence to publicly display their pricing, including their GPLs, casket price lists, and outer burial container price lists, wrote Becca Trate of the Center for Data Innovation.

It's an issue the FTC had been considering for more than three years, amid opposition by many in the industry who fear such a move would give their competitors a market advantage.

The Consumer Federation of America and the Funeral Consumers Alliance in 2022 urged the FTC to adopt this requirement, which would allow consumers to compare prices without having to visit each funeral home. Most consumers, especially older people, the less wealthy, and those out-of-town or having to deal with sudden death, can't practically visit several funeral homes to pick up price lists, they pointed out.

" If the internet had existed when the Funeral Rule was issued in 1984," the advocacy groups said, the rule would long ago have required online posting of price lists. But it appeared that funeral homes were actually trying to hide their price lists, while those that, in fact, did post them benefited by attracting customers.

An educated, motivated consumer, armed with FCA price material, is often able to bargain and get their bill knocked down. Determining priorities, comparison shopping, and understanding consumer rights can save money. Both groups have consistently urged the FTC to make changes to strengthen the Rule, but the FTC has still failed to do so at the publication of this book.

"Grief and pain associated with death should not be compounded by anxiety and costs in choosing funeral services," Rebecca Kelly Slaughter, one of four FTC members, told a workshop in September 2023.

Some have suggested the commission is more interested in accommodating the industry than in protecting the public.

A consumer advocate with the FCA, Jim Bates, who's had contact with thousands of consumers over 30 years, told the workshop that posting price lists on funeral home websites is clearly a control issue. "Consumers," Bates said, "know they have very little control over the process of displaying prices. But the industry very obviously wants to maintain that control."

He tries to teach students in college classes and seniors' groups how to gain control, including understanding the language of the process.

Another panellist recommended that consumers look for a source that earns their trust, not just price. Price listings should be in a readable, common language, not in 'funeral-speak', and price lists should include user-friendly words readable language at the third- and fourth-grade reading level.

Economists working for the UK Government's Competition and Markets Authority (CMA), who undertook an extensive investigation into the funeral industry in 2018-20, recommended introducing price caps on standard funeral packages.

But faced with concerns from funeral directors and crematoria that they continue to'earn an acceptable return, the authority reached the compromise of requiring businesses to display price information to consumers online. Since the CMA order was brought into effect in 2021, the Quaker Social Action web portal reported almost 250 funeral directors to the CMA for non-compliance. It also reported that "around a quarter" of funeral directors required to provide the CMA with financial information hadn't done so.

Pre-Payment Plans

The funeral industry's answer to paying for funerals and end-of-life arrangements is to pay it all in advance. That's no doubt in the industry's interests, much more than for millions of families. Paying ahead can help a family avoid stress and costs when needed, but a better option is to plan ahead and set money aside rather than paying in advance. Pre-paying usually simply means 'pay now and die poorer.'

Former Funeral Consumers Alliance executive director in 2012, Josh Slocum, told CBS 60 Minutes, "I cannot and will not recommend that most consumers pre-pay. This is standard advice from people who don't have an interest in selling to you, because hundreds of millions of dollars have gone missing, raided from funds over the past years. If you do feel you have to pre-pay, read the fine print carefully. Know how much you're entitled to a refund, if any, and if you move or change your mind, know whether the price is guaranteed and if any excess payment death after your death will be given to your survivors."

The American Association for Retired Persons and Consumer Reports agreed.

To be fair, in the same 60 Minutes program, Paul Elvig, the late president of the International Cemetery, Cremation and Funeral Association, pointed out that purchasing a grave and purchasing goods and services are two different stories. "In many states, if you go on public assistance, which many people end up having to do, if you don't already own a grave, the only disposition the state may pay for is cremation," he said. "Your best control is if you buy that grave in advance. It's something you can do together as a family."

Haneman also cautioned families about being duped or missing out on death benefits or tax incentives. She has encouraged families to engage in an all-out attack on the death care industry by using a section of the U.S. Internal Revenue Code to avoid leaving death care expenses to their heirs.

"It's important for the death care consumer to engage in pre-planning," she stressed. To avoid pre-paying funeral expenses, what she calls 'pay-now-die-later arrangements,' it's important to address funeral poverty.

"The easiest way to bear an 'unexpected expense' is to render it 'expected' and to make payments over time," Haneman recommended. In short, to expect the death of a family member or oneself.

The Future of Death Care

The funeral and death care industries, especially the big players, are long overdue for a complete overhaul, whether they like it or not. And it may be starting to happen.

Consumers are beginning to say it's time the corporate funeral sector started getting its collective noses out of the trough. Among major concerns are the cost of cemetery burial rising beyond affordability for many, and the environmental impacts of flame cremation, which uses the same amount of energy and has the same emissions as two tanks of gas in an average car.

Eco-friendly movements have begun to attract more and more people as they recognize the impact their bodies will have on the environment once they're gone. They're starting to realize that millions of pounds of metal, wood, and concrete are added to the ground to shield bodies from the surrounding earth.

More should be done to encourage people, particularly those with middle and low incomes, to prepare for death through simple guidance and advice from advocacy groups like memorial and consumer societies.

There's obviously a growing need for individuals and their families, along with society at large, to identify and encourage environmentally responsible alternative methods.

"The death care industry is as inescapable for most American families as death itself," Prof. Haneman said. "Putting the deceased to rest often carries unexpected funerary expenses for cremations, funerals, burials, and memorials." She's "highly supportive of 'absolutely everything' in terms of innovative death care and disposition technology.

Academics and consumer advocates alike deplore the cost to families of the end-of-life burden and what needs to be done to provide relief. Many among the public are now demanding just that. But too many are still willing to accept the excesses of the industry or simply don't realize there are alternatives, a regrettable and tragic lack of know-how on their part. Governments need to start approving new technologies for dealing with our dead before vastly larger numbers of baby boomers and the other older generations continue to depart.

"The alliance is well aware of funeral poverty," FCA President Williams said, "including problems of access and affordability when it comes to funeral expenses."

Local FCA affiliates, like hers in North Carolina, receive heartbreaking phone calls and emails every single week, sometimes daily, seeking financial help. Typically, she and the FCA offices get calls saying things like "My brother just died and we don't have money to pay for the funeral. We thought he had life insurance, but he didn't. We have to tell the caller that, unfortunately, the FCA, as a non-profit volunteer organization, doesn't have funds for any type of funeral assistance."

But, she said, she can help them think through how to save money and still do right by their relatives. "Stories like these highlight our responsibility to amplify our educational outreach," Williams explained.

On top of that, the U.S. government has perpetuated the myth that a funeral will likely cost thousands of dollars, Williams says. The American Rescue Plan included assistance of up to $9,000 for funeral expenses for a death caused by COVID-19.

When it comes to funeral poverty, Williams said (as diplomatically as she could), "Just the fact that people wait around and wait around and they don't plan for it... It's their burden. I don't say that in a mean or hateful way. But we've been telling you this. What are you thinking, leaving this mess for your family?"

The Tragedy of Unclaimed Bodies

Unfortunately, no amount of advance planning will help some of the deceased, those whose bodies are unclaimed.

In some cases, identification is difficult or impossible, so the families live unaware of the death of their loved ones. In other cases, families faced with unaffordable end-of-life costs for disposition by any means, burial, cremation, or more recent methods, simply don't claim the body. The rising costs of funeral services are, for many, simply out of the question.

Wired Magazine reported that, in the United States in 2021, as many as three percent of bodies are left unclaimed each year, a number that reportedly rose due to economic inequality, the opioid epidemic, and the pandemic. "In the worst-case scenario," it reported, "people will be forced to leave their loved ones unclaimed in county custody, where sheriffs, medical examiners, social workers, chaplains, and others will cremate or bury their remains."

"The treatment of unidentified bodies is a personal tragedy for families of the deceased who face the anguish of so-called ambiguous loss," the Lancet reported. "This psychological state, marked by uncertainty about the fate of the missing, has severe negative effects on an individual's wellbeing and health that makes identification of the dead a crucial global public health priority."

The problem surfaces everywhere.

In October of 2023, 189 decomposing bodies were removed from a Colorado funeral home. In January 2024, 215 bodies were found buried in unmarked graves behind a jail in Jackson, Mississippi, leaving the community in disbelief.

In four of Ontario's largest cities, Toronto, Hamilton, London, and Ottawa, the remains of 1,183 people went unclaimed in 2023. Provincial figures showed the number of bodies not claimed by family members had surged since 2019, when only 438 were reported.

In March of 2024, CBC reported that the Health Sciences Centre morgue in St. John's, Newfoundland and Labrador, had to install industrial freezers to hold about 28 unclaimed bodies in an alley just a few feet away from a garbage dumpster. Subsequently, the facility built three new walk-in freezer units in the underground garage to deal with the morgue's overflow of bodies. Provincial legislators said the families involved simply could not afford to pay funeral bills to have their loved ones buried or cremated. The province's health minister said anyone "with compassion would find it disturbing."

"While human identification is a crucial aspect of medico-legal investigations, many individuals remain unidentified each year across the world," the U.S. National Library of Medicine reported in 2023. It also reported that, on average, developing countries experienced more than double the number of unidentified bodies when compared to developed nations.

The most common issue faced is a lack of standardized procedures for forensic human identification. Such procedures include criminal investigation of death, which carries 'obvious value in the criminal justice sector.'

Families of the deceased are entitled to bury or cremate their loved ones, and in many cultures, this is to show respect for the deceased. Administratively, identification is necessary for the completion of the death certificate, which is further required for the release of life insurance policies and control of assets.

The lack of identification of a body not only prevents the reunion of the deceased with their loved ones but also indicates the family and community are unaware of that individual's death.

That places strain, both financially and logistically, on state facilities to store or bury the remains.

When they were alive, many of these people were marginalized due to social and health inequalities, undocumented migrants, members of disadvantaged minority ethnic groups, people of colour, the urban poor and homeless, individuals with severe mental illness, addictions, and other stigmatized groups.

The extremely high number of unidentified bodies, the Lancet said, has been referred to as 'a silent mass disaster.'

Chapter 13: The Wages of Wealth – The Death Care Industry

"I, like most independent funeral directors, don't like corporate-run funeral homes. I think they're bad for consumers, and consumers and they hurt the already injured perception of the funeral industry by perpetuating the money-hungry mortician stereotype." – Caleb Wilde, Parkesburg, Pennsylvania (Confessions of a Funeral Director, 2017)

The global death care market had reached $104 billion a year by 2020. It was expected to soar to $189.9 billion by 2030, an annual growth rate of 6.1 percent.

For years, the death care industry has been haunted by revelations of sharp practices and extreme profit-seeking. Indeed, the Victorian trope of the greedy funeral director, often a wealthy miser lacking scruples and motivated only by money, is still with us today. Ripping people off at sad and vulnerable moments in their lives is beyond reproach, but not beyond reality.

It's not news that the multi-billion-dollar corporate death care sector uses slick and often questionable sales practices, upselling products and services to boost sales and prices.

Costs have gotten even steeper because of the ongoing consolidation of funeral homes and cemeteries in recent years by corporate chains and private equity firms.

The biggest in the corporate death care sector by far is Service Corporation International (SCI). SCI serves about 450,000 customers a year. It had $4.19 billion in revenues for the year 2024, a 2.1 percent increase from 2023. Its 2024 fourth-quarter revenues alone increased $37 million, or 4 percent, over the same quarter of 2023. That compares with 1995 revenues of over $1.5 billion and 15,000 employees. Its present assets are $15.6 billion.

Not everyone has to deal with the corporate giants. The National Funeral Directors Association (NFDA) is the world's leading and largest funeral service association, serving 19,700 individual members who represent more than 10,000 funeral homes in the United States and 49 countries around the world.

The late director of the U.S. Funeral Ethics Organization, Lisa Carlson, said the big players tend to view the death industry as a cash cow and often operate with monthly quotas and revenue targets. They are usually more expensive than family-owned companies or co-operatives, and they have a reputation for dubious business practices that often leave people looking for alternatives.

Independent family or co-op owned-and-operated funeral homes generally take pride in their services and spend less time 'upselling' services and products. Turning a profit is part of the equation. But their staff aren't normally required to meet sales quotas. It might be a stretch to imagine the big guns of the "dismal trade" rubbing their hands in anticipation of the end of a baby boom generation. But their focus continues to be more on price points and corporate returns than on grieving families.

Funeral homes owned by corporations are still the minority of the roughly 20,000 homes in the United States, 1,700 in Canada, and 7,000 in the United Kingdom, but they've been by far the fastest-growing segment of the market.

Caleb Wilde's opinion was shared by long-retired funeral director Darryl Roberts, who wrote in his 1997 book *Profits of Death* that, for years, giant corporations have been gobbling up the independent funeral homes at a "voracious" rate.

"The buying-power advantage of a conglomerate is obvious," Roberts wrote. "But if a conglomerate has control of an entire segment of the market, will those savings be passed on to the consumer? That doesn't appear to be the case."

Since its founding in 1962, SCI has bought out hundreds of family-owned funeral homes. Headquartered near Houston, Texas, it operates under several names with close to 1,488 funeral homes and 491 cemeteries in 44 U.S. states, eight Canadian provinces, the UK, Puerto Rico, and a myriad of other countries. The bulk of its revenue is generated by operations in the U.S. and Canada. It operates in Canada as Dignity Memorial and in the UK as Dignity Plc. Though some media describe SCI as 'the Walmart' of the funeral industry, the comparison doesn't quite hold.

"Unlike Walmart, SCI's economies of scale don't translate into cost savings for consumers," the Funeral Consumers Alliance said. A survey conducted by the FCA and the Consumer Federation of America revealed that SCI's median prices are "significantly higher" than independently owned funeral homes.

'Funeralgate' and 'Formaledegate'

SCI was involved in a 1990s controversy involving alleged violations of embalming laws in Texas. This became a political issue due to a company executive's friendship with (and contributions to) the family of then-governor and later president George W. Bush. The media, inevitably, dubbed it 'Funeralgate' (or 'Formaldegate'). A lawsuit against SCI over the alleged violations was settled for $200,000.

Around the same time, it was revealed that workers at SCI's Memorial Gardens cemetery near Fort Lauderdale, Florida, buried people in the wrong places, broke open vaults to squeeze in other remains, and, in some instances, tossed bones into the woods. Bodies were stacked on top of each other, and remains were relocated without notifying relatives. The cemetery employees had oversold plots and run out of space.

The allegations particularly appalled observant Jewish customers. (Under Jewish law, bodies must be buried intact and undisturbed.)

SCI agreed to settle the Fort Lauderdale suit for $100 million, distributed among 350 families and their lawyers. In addition to that payout, SCI reached a $14 million agreement with the state attorney general's office that required the company to repair the plots and reorganize the cemeteries to ensure graves were properly marked and could be accommodated.

The Washington Post ran a series about SCI in the early 2000s. One story was about the burial of a stillborn child in a grave just 8 inches (20 centimeters) deep. Another reported that an SCI facility was storing decomposing naked bodies in "disgusting, degrading, and humiliating" conditions. Among the hundreds of bodies stored on makeshift gurneys and shelves in an unrefrigerated garage were deceased veterans awaiting burial at Arlington National Cemetery.

A 2009 class-action suit against SCI and a Jewish cemetery it managed, Eden Memorial Park in Mission Hills, California, alleged that managers at the cemetery broke as many as 1,500 buried concrete vaults in order to fit in more bodies and discarded or lost human skulls and other remains in a "dump area." SCI denied wrongdoing but agreed to a settlement of $80.5 million.

Yahoo News, in September 2022, reported that SCI's cremation services agreed to pay up to $209 million in refunds to settle a federal class-action lawsuit alleging it deceived 87,000 Florida customers who purchased its prepaid plans. SCI Direct Inc., formerly called Neptune Society Management Corp., was named as a co-defendant in the class action.

The class action accused the companies of violating Florida laws that require prepaid cremation services providers to deposit 70 percent of prepaid funds into a trust and provide 100 percent refunds upon request. It also accused the companies of unjust enrichment and violations of the state's Deceptive and Unfair Trade Practices Act.

SCI is hardly alone among large funeral chains to be accused of dubious practices. In April 2022, the U.S. Department of Justice, acting on behalf of the Federal Trade Commission, announced that it was suing Funeral & Cremation Group of North America, Legacy Cremation Services and Heritage Cremation Provider, among others, for "misrepresenting their location and prices, illegally threatening and failing to return cremated remains to consumers and failing to provide disclosures required by the (U.S.) Funeral Rule."

The defendants, according to the DOJ suit, frequently posed as local providers when they weren't and charged consumers more than their posted prices. When consumers resisted undisclosed fees and price increases, the companies in question allegedly held the remains hostage. Said Samuel Levine, director of the FTC's Bureau of Consumer Protection, "Preying on consumers when they are dealing with the loss of a loved one is outrageous and it's illegal."

The Funeral Rule mentioned in the DOJ suit was enacted by the U.S. Federal Trade Commission (FTC) in 1984 and updated a decade later. It was inspired, in part, by Jessica Mitford's 1963 bestseller *The American Way of Death*, revised in a 2000 edition, that documented the many ways in which funeral directors took advantage of grieving friends and family to convince them to overpay for services. Mitford's investigations brought changes to American law designed to protect consumers from unscrupulous practitioners.

"The Rule," as it's known, is intended to protect consumers from unethical and often outrageous practices by giving consumers adequate information about services and products, including pricing and so-called "pre-need" arrangements.

Under the Funeral Rule, funeral directors are required to provide their price lists to families at the beginning of funeral discussions. It stipulates that a funeral home cannot insist that a customer buy a funeral package or pay for everything included in a package. It must make a full price list available on request, including the costs of lower-priced urns and caskets. A funeral home cannot refuse a casket or urn purchased elsewhere, nor charge a fee for the use of a casket or urn purchased elsewhere. A casket is not required for cremation, and a funeral home cannot require one.

Consumers have the right to purchase services and products item-by-item, selecting only what they need. They have the right to decline embalming. They are free to call around to other funeral homes seeking better prices or services.

The intent of the Funeral Rule is to "address the imbalance between the buyer, who is grieving, and the vendor, who is in a rational and businesslike frame of mind," says the Funeral Consumers Alliance. The FCA advises individuals and families to take a realistic look at their budgets before calling a funeral home and deciding what they can reasonably afford without sacrificing funds for daily living.

The alliance has repeatedly urged the Federal Trade Commission to give The Rule more teeth. "The funeral industry's reluctance to operate transparently and competitively will not be remedied without more effective and up-to-date government regulations," it says.

Few other countries have adopted similar regulations to the Funeral Rule. But dubious practices by corporate funeral giants are by no means unique to the United States. They're rife in countries where governments tend to take a largely hands-off approach to the industry.

Australia's $1 billion (AUD) funeral sector is not immune to shady players. Whitsunday Funeral and Crematorium is a family-owned business that operates funeral homes in Queensland. It is regarded as one of the most reputable in the area. But owner Jeff Boyle had little good to say about some of his competitors. In a television interview, Boyle claimed that many facilities use fake tops to cover cheap coffins used for cremations. Some, he said, switch coffins at the last minute, often with pine or fiberboard boxes, without informing customers.

"Absolutely disgraceful," said the consumer advocacy group CHOICE, which investigated consumer rip-offs in Australia's funeral industry. Its report also detailed wide discrepancies in pricing among providers.

In 2017, the Canadian Broadcasting Corporation's (CBC) Marketplace program and The Toronto Star newspaper undertook a joint investigation of Arbor Memorial, the largest funeral home chain in Canada.

It found markups on caskets and urns averaged 185 percent, depending on the model, and, in some cases, nearly 500 percent.

These calculations were based on retail prices at 23 Arbor Memorial homes in southern Ontario and a wholesale price list from one large manufacturer.

Posing as relatives, reporters were shown packages for pre-arranged funerals "featuring essential services, such as funeral co-ordination and transferring the body, as well as discretionary services, such as catering, stationery, cars for transporting flowers and chapel staffing."

Arbor salespeople stated directly to the undercover reporters that all the items, or the vast majority, were necessary. Among the fees was a $340 (CAD) charge to transport a body from a funeral home to a crematorium –on the same property.

Arbor said in a statement at the time that its packaged funeral services provide "good value," are easy to understand, and offer savings. It said an "à la carte" approach is an option. The reporters found that even prices quoted by SCI were lower than those from Arbor.

Arbor Memorial also has a leading market share in British Columbia, although SCI controls 54 percent of all funeral homes in the populous lower mainland, said death care coach Stephen Garrett, who was previously employed by The Memorial Society of British Columbia.

Garrett learned a lot about how the big firms operate while employed earlier by SCI: "If you want to see the devil's eyes, get close to him. I lasted a year and a half, and I quit. I actually got fired because I was too nice."

Corporate 'Funeral Monsters'

Critics like funeral director Caleb Wilde admit that the "corporate monsters" make contributions to the profession. For example, they offer funeral directors an opportunity to find their first job, often pay better, and offer more days off and vacation time, provided the employee meets company sales quotas. Nevertheless, consumers should research who they're dealing with.

There's normally a clear difference between genuine, independent, family-owned, or co-op funeral homes and the big chains. The giants of the industry often masquerade under the names of small "economy" funeral homes, so it's important to find out if the firm has an investment in the local community or whether it's answerable to an often-distant board of directors.

Death care consultant Shane Neufeld, who's worked for both big and small players, said that the chains don't have a monopoly on bad behavior. "All the things that I saw going on that were the worst tactics were always in privately-owned establishments," he said. "Just because they're independent doesn't mean they're scrupulous."

Neufeld argued that there are some inhibitions on bad behavior at the big firms that don't pertain to smaller operations. Employees at the chains are expected to adhere to policy manuals that are designed to insulate them from lawsuits. "If anything's going on that's a liability to the organization," Neufeld said," they want to nip that in the bud. They fear litigation, and they have a lot to lose."

"I used to be a corporate finance guy, and I know how the corporate mind works," Garrett said. "They see a million baby boomers in BC and that's times $10,000. That's a $10-billion dollar payday. So that's what's going on."

The quest for higher returns and big paydays keeps prices generally higher at the corporate funeral chains, and they've been known to increase by as much as 10 percent a year. Grieving families are subjected to aggressive sales pitches for high-end services, caskets, and other arrangements.

Costs Continue to Rise

A UK study authored in 2020 by Professors Samantha Fletcher and William McGowan found the funeral industry "has evolved in such a way that costs have risen continually, often in quite deliberate and manipulated ways."

Huge corporate providers have "greedy shareholder mouths to feed," said McGowan, and "natural and commensurate supply and demand is too modest, financially speaking. So they have to work hard to create and capitalize on greater demand by not only pursuing the dead but targeting the living as well."

The largest funeral service provider in the market is Dignity PLC (the UK arm of SCI). It has a total of 700 branches with plans for further expansion. More than 350 subsidiaries, most of them formerly independent morticians bought out by Dignity, have retained their traditional family-run names. Dignity is also the largest operator among the 283 crematoria in the United Kingdom.

Chapter 14: Universal Death Care – To Be or Not To Be?

"I like the idea of removing profit altogether from the death care industry." – Hunter Beattie, North Carolina, Funeral Home Owner

Dying can be a costly business, and those costs can hit the unprepared at the lower end of the economic spectrum particularly hard.

But some governments do have programs available to soften the financial blow to the deceased's loved ones or to cover funeral expenses. In Canada, individuals can't deduct funeral expenses, but eligible estates may be able to claim a deduction if the estate paid these costs. Effective January 2025, the amount of death benefit for the estate or eligible survivors under the Canada Pension Plan and the Quebec Pension Plan is a basic amount of $2,500 and a possible top-up of $2,500, for a maximum benefit is $5,000.

In the UK, death benefits primarily consist of the Bereavement Support Payment, which offers a lump sum of £3,500 and monthly payments of £350 for 18 months to surviving partners, with higher rates for those responsible for children. Funeral Expenses Payments are also available for low-income individuals. Eligibility and rates of compensation are dependent on one's National Insurance record.

In Australia, a death benefit refers to a payment made from a deceased person's superannuation account (regular payments made into a fund by an employee toward a future pension) to their dependent beneficiaries, which can be a lump sum or over time, and is generally tax-free. To be eligible to receive this Bereavement Allowance, you must meet an income and assets test. Australia does have programs to help with funeral costs, but they vary by state and territory.

New Zealand provides a one-off payment of $7,531.49 to the deceased's spouse or partner and a one-off payment of $3,765.76 to each child under 18 or other dependents, if the death was accidental. A Funeral Grant of up to $2,616.12 is available if the estate of the person who has died can't pay. This money can be used for costs such as professional services for preparing the body for cremation or burial.

In the United States, a death benefit under Social Security is a one-time lump-sum payment of $255 to an eligible spouse or, in some cases, children, upon the death of a Social Security-insured worker. Many states and local governments assist low-income families who cannot afford funerals. These programs vary by location but often provide financial aid to cover basic burial or cremation costs.

Sweden Sets the Standard

None of these programs compares to what is provided in Sweden. The Swedish government in 1990 implemented what it calls a burial tax that covers the cost of disposition. Everyone registered in the population registry pays a mandatory burial fee (begravningsavgift) through their income taxes. This fee covers the costs of maintaining cemeteries, cremation, burial, and other related services. The burial fee is not linked to individual funeral arrangements but rather funds the overall infrastructure and services related to death and burial.

If the deceased was a member of the Church of Sweden, the cost of the funeral ceremony, including the officiant and music, may be covered by the church fee. Those not members of the Church of Sweden can still have a funeral ceremony, but it may involve additional costs for the services of a religious leader or celebrant. The deceased's estate typically covers the costs of the funeral ceremony, including the choice of venue and any specific arrangements beyond the basic services covered by the burial fee. The County Administrative Board in every Swedish county and municipality is required to appoint a funeral ombudsman for people who are not members of the Church of Sweden.

Universal Death Care

Tax-funded death care is not an entirely new concept, though the likelihood of it being realized in a time of high costs and fiscal restraint makes it indeed unlikely in the foreseeable future.

Universal healthcare has been a fixture of life in the United Kingdom since its introduction by a Labour Government in 1948. Since then, no UK prime minister, including the late arch-conservative Margaret Thatcher, has ventured to lay hands on the National Health Service (NHS), at least until recently. Many in the UK continue to unite in one voice: Hands off our NHS.

But for a relatively modest £2 billion a year added to the NHS budget of £200 billion, the UK could offer access to universal death care, William McGowan, a lecturer at Liverpool John Moores University, contends. That figure is based on an anticipated annual death toll of 500,000 and the average cost of a basic funeral pegged at around £4,000 (c.$5,000 USD).

A national service run for people rather than profit could source and distribute materials and services at a much more competitive rate than the corporate sector if there was the political will to do so, and now might be a perfect time to do it, McGowan said. "Universal funeral care should be our aspiration... absolutely. The state can and should cover the costs of us leaving this world."

"Funds for funerals could come from a combination of income tax and national insurance," he said, "raising the possibility of nationalizing the industry. A national death care service could provide an adequate and respectable level of care and service through the NHS, adding people could still make private arrangements."

"Regulating the freewheeling funeral industry has always been on the back burner, let alone talk of nationalizing the industry altogether," McGowan said, noting that corporate providers have exacerbated the cost of funerals by pushing up prices consistently for 20 years, then capitalizing on this by selling pre-need arrangements.

However, universal death care would be an even longer shot in the United States, certainly in the political atmosphere of the early 2020s.

Professor Philip Olson, a technology ethicist at Virginia Polytechnic, contends that a federally funded death care program should be seriously considered as a goal of U.S. society. End-of-life costs, he said, should be paid for out of taxes, possibly through an eventual adoption of 'Medicare for all,' if only for those over 65. Alternatively, Olson said, it could be funded by several sources, mostly payroll taxes. Death care programs in the U.S. could cover essential costs of a coffin or other end-of-life services for everyone, including natural burial, aquamation, or human composting to ensure the dignity of all humans.

"But the idea of a 'socialized' death care system for some is likely to be just too... well, 'socialist,'" Olson admitted. Some even argue that a universal death care program would instead benefit a corporate funeral/death care industry.

Victoria Haneman, for one, doesn't share Olson's hope of a universal death care program taking root in the U.S., at least not in recent political climates. "You can come up with an idea and it's never going to happen," the Creighton University professor said.

"In the United States, initiatives with the word 'universal 'before them don't succeed in the political process," she said. "People don't want to talk about such a plan," she told a 2024 symposium on future death care. "At a time of escalating healthcare, education, and housing costs, death care as a universal initiative is viewed as 'socialist,'" Haneman said. "Universal death care as a branded product would be disastrous for the politician who pitches it."

The U.S. offers several programs that allow employees to earmark deductions from their paychecks for healthcare expenses and, at the same time, lower taxable income. They could easily be extended or copied to include death care, she said.

Under her proposal, a taxpayer would sign up for a flexible spending account through their employer that lets them set aside a portion of their earnings. The money then compounds over time, and qualified expenses are reimbursed without compound interest being taxed.

"The idea is that the consumer commits to contemplating an 'undesirable subject' (their death) in exchange for a reward, which is federal tax-sharing of the death care expense," Haneman said. "Making such an arrangement is not just an incentive; it's also consumer protection," she argued. "That should have the effect of reforming a death care industry that's been doing things the same way for almost a hundred years."

She said the use of such a tax subsidy that would help the most vulnerable among us is something that's capable of getting bipartisan political support.

Taking the Money-Making Out of Death Care

In North Carolina in mid-2023, funeral home director Hunter Beattie launched his stand-alone service providing water-based cremation, or aquamation service, which later evolved into a full-service provider. Unlike most death care businesses, Endswell was barely breaking even at first. But he expected his company to be profitable within five years.

Hunter Beattie, owner of Endswell Funeral Home,
argues that death care should be a public service.

On the other hand, he'd like to see all death care taken over by local governments, counties, or states, starting with Hillsborough, where he does business. Beattie deplored the fact that death care is a money-making enterprise, even if he's a small part of it right now.

"The fact is, we all die," he said. "It's one of the things that happens to all of us, and the best way to deal with this is green burial and aquamation. So why are all these families being burdened? I like the idea of removing profit altogether from the death care industry."

Community-owned cemeteries used to be a normal feature of community life, but they are now mostly full, said Beattie, urging a return to that practice. Ideally, in Beattie's vision, every town or city would have its own bio-cremation machines and a green burial ground outside of town where one could take transit to visit loved ones. "When you die, you should just be aquamated and your tax dollars cover the cost," he said.

Beattie realizes he's a bit of an idealist. But he thinks the seed of his idea can't do any harm, and just might lead to something. "The problem is," he acknowledged, "the trend is in another direction, including privately-owned cemeteries."

"Current neoliberal capitalism is really commodifying everything, even for-profit prisons," he said. But he can see communities eventually getting behind non-profit or government-funded funeral homes, or the next-best thing, not-for-profit memorial societies, which are already a reality.

So, for him, it's more than just a dream.

A 2019 investigation by the UK Competition and Marketing Authority into soaring industry costs compared to profits for Dignity with other UK operators and companies in Europe, the United States, Canada, and Australia. Dignity recorded operating profits of between 19 and 26 percent, while those at Acorn AG in Germany and Park Lawn Corporation in Canada were between 13 and 16 percent. In 2021, SCI had a profit margin of 28 percent.

The phrase 'you despicable beasts' was one of many pieces of consumer invective quoted by Fletcher and McGowan in their study. They found plenty of evidence of public outrage at the practices and expense of the death care industry, but also that policy-makers tend to sidestep the issues.

Given the abundance of bad press, many are now suspicious of death care practices, particularly those of the big funeral chains. Unless significant changes are made, more and more people will look to bypass the industry altogether. The burden on lower-income families raises the admittedly controversial question of whether the state should fund or subsidize death care services. Whether such measures are warranted, or indeed, would be acceptable to the public, remains to be debated.

Postscript – Final Thoughts

"Why do people have to die?"

That was the question put by a bereaved family member to funeral director Nate Fisher in the award-winning HBO series *Six Feet Under*, praised as 'an unexpectedly beautiful rumination on life, death and grief.'

After pausing a moment to grasp a spark of wisdom, Nate responded in the most profound manner he could muster: "To make life important. None of us knows how long we've got, which is why we have to make each day matter. A life well-lived... that's the most any of us can hope for."

"Philosophers and theologians from around the globe have recognized the value that death holds for human life," The Lancet medical journal has written. "Death and life are bound together: without death, there would be no life. Death allows new ideas and new ways. Death also reminds us of our fragility and sameness: we all die."

Why This Book?

This is doubtless the last book the author will write on this delicate but important subject. An earlier one preceded it, but the subject required a fresh look and several updates.

Oddly enough, it is the only book that, to date, covers the subject in an inclusive and, the author likes to think, as accurate, fair, and comprehensive a manner as possible.

A number of excellent books were consulted, but none of them were comprehensive or up-to-date. Meanwhile, I've received valuable guidance from many individuals knowledgeable about the subject and with open minds about the future of death care.

Most of us would prefer to avoid having to deal with the deaths of loved ones, but it is an inescapable obligation. And families must confront these decisions while faced with inevitable inflationary costs. The book's primary intention is to be helpful to family members in making these decisions. And there are now new affordable and eco-friendly options for making these choices.

At the time of publication of this book, cremation by flame remained the most widely accepted method in most Western countries, but extremely detrimental to the environment due to emissions of CO_2 and other pollutants. But, as the book suggests, that will soon change with newer technology that has become available within this century.

The author is the last surviving member of his own original core family, a typical scenario. My grandparents on both sides were born in the mid-1800s, died between the 1930s and early 1960s, and were buried in cemeteries near my hometown. My parents in the 1970s wisely made their own decisions for the eventual ends of their lives. Their choice was cremation. Both my sisters died in the early 2000s and had made the same decision. I've chosen to donate my body to the closest medical school, if they'll still have me. My preferred choice would be cremation by water (as dealt with in Chapter 1). But I won't be around to either know or care.

"Be now forever taken from my sight. Though nothing can bring back the hour of splendour in the grass, of glory in the flower; We will grieve not, rather find Strength in what remains behind." – Ode from Intimations of Immortality. William Wordsworth, 1770-1850

"The reality is that you will grieve forever. You will not 'get over' the loss of a loved one; you will learn to live with it. You will heal and you will rebuild yourself around the loss you have suffered. You will be whole again but you will never be the same. Nor should you the name nor would you want to." – Elizabeth Kubler-Ross, Swiss-American Psychiatrist, 1926-2004

Addendum 1: Membership-Based Movements

Memorial societies and funeral co-operatives, going back to the 1920s, evolved with different roles to provide guidance and advice to their members on planning the most cost-effective funerals. They later developed as a way of combating the growing corporate sector in the death care industry.

The difference is that memorial societies, as non-profit entities, collaborate with funeral homes to provide simple, dignified, and cost-effective funerals. They can result in lower-cost services. Funeral co-ops have a similar goal but take a different approach to running the funeral companies owned by their members. Both require planning for the practicalities and costs of future death and offer the opportunity for members to save for their families.

In the 1960s, a national funeral consumer movement emerged from these beginnings, the Funeral Consumers Alliance (FCA).

With member branches throughout the United States, similar to cooperatives and memorial associations in both the U.S. and Canada, the FCA is dedicated to protecting consumer rights and dignified, affordable funerals. With the help of its members, it conducts price surveys of funeral homes and negotiates discounts with affiliated homes. The FCA affiliates are among about 70 non-profit funeral planning groups in the U.S. (see Addendum 2)

The FCA is to the funeral industry what Consumer Reports is to the general consumer industry, Tom Barlow wrote in Forbes magazine, describing it as a source of objective information.

San Francisco lawyer Bob Treuhaft and his journalist wife Jessica Mitford, the author who caused a stir with her top-selling *The American Way of Death*, founded one of the oldest affiliates, the Bay Area Funeral Society. They were on the founding board that created the FCA in 1963 as the Continental Association of Funeral and Memorial Societies (CAFMS). (Canadian memorial societies were part of the federation but separated in the 1980s and '90s because of differing national laws.)

The association helped the Federal Trade Commission write the first national regulations in the 1970s, giving consumers the right to buy only what they want, as well as itemized price lists, the right to price quotes by phone, and to buy outside merchandise. The Funeral Rule went into effect in 1984.

In 1999, the board renamed the association the Funeral Consumers Alliance. The state-level chapters of the FCA are dedicated to helping individuals and families make informed and cost-effective choices regarding funeral arrangements. They operate on the principle of consumer advocacy, aiming to ensure that people have access to affordable and dignified funeral options.

FCA chapters are non-profit entities whose primary focus is serving the interests of their members rather than generating profits. Joining a chapter typically involves paying a membership fee. In return, members gain access to resources, educational materials, and discounted funeral services. This includes providing educational programs and workshops to inform members about their rights, choices, and the legal aspects of funeral planning. They offer guidance on available options and work to ensure fair and transparent pricing. The local affiliates or chapters tailor their services to the needs and regulations of their respective communities.

They conduct surveys of local funeral homes to compile price lists for various services to help members compare costs and make financially responsible choices. Some also negotiate discounts with funeral homes for their members.

The chapters may assist members in preplanning their funerals, making decisions about the type of service, burials, or other disposition preferences. This empowers individuals to make well-informed decisions when arranging funerals or preplanning for future needs.

FCA Chapters:

Arizona FCA of Arizona, Tucson (520-721-0230) director@fcaaz.org www.fcaaz.org

California San Diego Memorial Society (858-391-1267) office@sdmsonline.com https://sdmsonline.com

Colorado Funeral Consumer Society of Colorado (720-432-5379) fucosoco@yahoo.com www.funeralconsumercolorado.org

Connecticut FCA of Connecticut (860-355-4197) info@funeralsct.org www.funeralsct.org

Delaware (Served by FCA of Maryland & Environs)

FCA of Suncoast Florida (941-953-3740) FCASuncoastFL@gmail.com www.FCASuncoastFL.com

FCA of Georgia (770-580-0655) info@fcaga.org www.fcaga.org

FCA of Idaho (208-426-0032) fcai-info@fortboise.org www.fcai.fortboise.org

FCA of Champaign County, Illinois fcaccil1@gmail.com https://funeralschampaigncounty.org

FCA of Greater Kansas City (816-561-6322) fca.gkc@gmail.com www.funeralskc.org

Louisiana (Served by FCA of North Texas)

FCA of Maine (207-558-1699) info@fcamaine.net www.fcamaine.net

FCA of Maryland & Environs info@mdfunerals.org https://mdfunerals.org

FCA of Eastern Massachusetts (Also serves central Massachusetts) (617-859-7990) info@fcaemass.org www.fcaemass.org

FCA of Western Massachusetts, MA (413-376-4747) fcawmass@gmail.com www.funeralconsumerswmass.org

Missouri FCA of Greater Kansas City (816-561-6322) fca.gkc@gmail.com www.funeralskc.org

New Hampshire (No FCA Affiliate) For education, advocacy, and price survey by Lee Webster: (603-236-9495) nhfrea@gmail.com https://www.nhfuneral.org/

New Jersey FCA of Princeton (609-924-3320) info@fcaprinceton.org https://www.fcaprinceton.org/ Laurie Powsner, contact (609-577-1948) lrpjak@gmail.com

FCA of Northern New Jersey (973-346-2423) fcannj@gmail.com www.fcannj.org

FCA of the Finger Lakes, Ithaca, NY (607-229-5286) info@fingerlakesfunerals.org www.fingerlakesfunerals.org

FCA of the Hudson Valley, Poughkeepsie, NY (609-232-2608) fcahv@fcahv.org www.fcahv.org

FCA of Greater Rochester, NY (585-461-1620) funeralalliancerochester@gmail.com www.fcagr.com

FCA of Central New York, DeWitt (315-446-0557) fcacny@gmail.com www.fcacny.org

Greater Buffalo Memorial Society, Amherst (716-244-1856) gbms.wny@gmail.com

North Carolina FCA, Wilmington, NC (984-464-0120) funeralsnc.org@gmail.com www.funeralsnc.org

FCA of the Central Carolinas, Charlotte (704-996-4524) funeralconsumersalliancecc@gmail.com

Ohio Cleveland Memorial Society, Shaker Heights (216-751-5515) info@clevememorialsociety.org www.clevememorialsociety.org

FCA of Central Ohio, Columbus (614-263-4632) info@funeralsohio.org www.funeralsohio.org

Oklahoma (Served by FCA of North Texas)

Oregon Memorial Association (503-647-5590) omaoregon@gmail.com www.omaoregon.org

FCA of Pennsylvania (267-712-9695) fcapennsylvania@gmail.com www.fcapa.org

FCA of Western PA, Pittsburgh (412-241-0705) info@funeralconsumerswpa.org

FCA of Rhode Island, East Greenwich (401-884-1131) Fcainri@gmail.com www.funerals-ri.org

South Carolina FCA of SC, Columbia (803-343-9090) Scfunerals@gmail.com www.scfunerals.org

Tennessee FCA of the Mid-South, Memphis (901-340-5259) furnissh@aol.com www.funeralcams.org

Texas FCA of Central Texas, Austin (512-480-0555) office@fcactx.org www.fcactx.org Exec. Dir.: Nancy Walker (512-480-0251) execdir@fcactx.org

FCA of North Texas, Fort Worth (972-509-5686) info@fcant.org fcant.org

FCA of San Antonio, TX (210-341-2213) Fcasatx9@gmail.com https://www.funeralssatx.org

FCA of Utah (801-368-5884) fcaofutah@gmail.com www.utahfunerals.org

Virginia FCA of The Virginia Blue Ridge (540-953-5589) fcavbr@gmail.com www.fcavbr.org

Washington People's Memorial Association, Seattle, (206-325-0489) https://peoplesmemorial.org/ info@peoplesmemorial.org

Wisconsin FCA of the Fox Valley (920-725-6880)
Ehudak71@gmail.com funeralsfoxvalley.com

FCA of Greater Milwaukee, Brookfield (414-731-3805)
fcaogm@gmail.com www.funeralswi.org

Funeral Consumers Alliance President Sara Williams
sara@funerals.org

NOTE: New FCA affiliates are being started in
Alabama, Arkansas, Chicago, Chattanooga, and Davenport-
Quad Cities. Readers may consult the FCA website
(fca@funerals.org) for up-to-date listings.

Memorial Societies, Funeral Co-Operatives:

Fighting inequality in the contemporary funeral industry.
All Equal in Death is a 2017 paper by professors at Laval
University in Quebec and the School of Administration in
Grenoble, France, which examined how alternative
economic organisations can fight inequality in the death care
sector. The paper focused on funeral co-operatives'
successful battle against corporate dominance of the funeral
industry in Quebec, where private enterprise and
multinational companies threatened to control the entire
sector. The report said high profits come from increased
expenses for families, who've been encouraged to spend
more on funerals.

In contrast to private enterprises, co-op members have
equal voting rights and member benefits. Co-ops are allowed
to make profits, but are limited in how they can distribute
them, with part returned to members and the remaining
excess reinvested in the co-op.

The membership-based organizations meet families' needs, regardless of spending ability, promote education, and encourage members to make funeral arrangements in advance. They're democratic organizations controlled by members who establish policies and make decisions.

The Minnesota Valley Funeral Home has been in operation for nearly a century. The funeral co-op was founded in 1929 in the small city of New Ulm, Minnesota, to provide affordable burials during the Great Depression. It has 5,000 members and still charges $5 for membership. As of 2021, it hadn't raised its prices for funerals in more than four years. Its profits, after costs, are shared with members who use the service in any given year. Like other co-ops, its members vote on how it operates. The director of the co-op in New Ulm, Eric Warmka, says his organisation has been getting more calls for information on how to fund and run a co-op.

The non-profit Peoples Memorial Association has served the greater Seattle area in Washington State since 1939. With a 2024 membership of over 90,000, it is the largest single co-op in North America. It contracts with funeral homes across the state to provide members with discounted funeral and cremation services. A lifetime membership costs $50 with no annual premiums. It has recently expanded its reach statewide by merging with its sister organisations, the Memorial Society of Central Washington and the Spokane Memorial Association.

Outraged by the steep prices and high-pressure sales tactics of the corporate funeral home industry, the members of Peoples Memorial decided in 2007 to open their own funeral home in response to the giant Service Corporation International purchasing locally owned funeral homes in the region. SCI increased prices and cancelled contracts that the association previously had with these businesses.

The People's Memorial conducts funeral home price surveys every two years in the state. It found the cost of cremation ranges from $600 to over $4,000. Some funeral homes were charging from $5,000 to over $15,000 for a burial, not including the cost of a cemetery plot and casket. It supported the legalization of alternatives to burial and cremation, such as alkaline hydrolysis and natural organic reduction or composting in Washington State.

In Canada, all provinces except Saskatchewan and Manitoba have funeral co-ops.

The Federation of Funeral Cooperatives of Quebec is an umbrella organisation for over 30 individual co-ops, representing 225,000 people. Twenty of the co-operatives are in Quebec. Others are located in Ontario and the Maritime provinces of New Brunswick, Nova Scotia, and Prince Edward Island, the U.S., France, Peru, and Costa Rico. With a combined total of 170,000 members. The largest Quebec funeral co-operative is in Quebec City, with over 25,000 members. Federation headquarters are in Sherbrooke, QC.

The Memorial Society of British Columbia, founded in 1956, has 250,000 members, the largest consumer advocacy group in Canada. The Co-operative Memorial Society in Alberta has served 46,000 members in the Calgary area since its creation in 1965.

In Ontario, the Funeral Advisory and Memorial Society (FAMS) has participating funeral homes and/or transfer services in Ajax, Barrie, Bowmanville, Brampton, Cobourg, Colborne, Cookstown, Kitchener, Newcastle, Oakville, Orangeville, Oshawa, Ottawa, Peterborough, and Toronto. Information is also available concerning funeral providers within Hamilton, Kitchener-Waterloo, and other parts of Southern Ontario. The Funeral Co-operative of Ottawa has a bilingual staff and offers aquamation.

Sunrise Funeral Co-operative was incorporated in 2024 to convert Newfoundland and Labrador funeral homes into not-for-profit, community-owned, and locally governed funeral community service co-operatives.

Canadian co-ops "didn't like the idea of big U.S. funeral corporations profiting from the deaths of Quebecers or Canadians," says Louis Grenier, secretary of the Calgary-based Alberta Cooperative Memorial Society. While two co-ops in Quebec bought out funeral homes from Service Corporation International, most of them don't own funeral homes, but purchase services from other independents.

Memorial Societies in the U.S.:

People's Memorial Association
info@peoplesmemorial.org

The National Memorial for Peace and Justice, Montgomery, Alabama, legacysites@eji.org (334-386-9100)

California Hospice and Palliative Care Association (916-925-3770) Email: info@calhospice.org

Georgia Byron Herbert Reece Society (706-379-4313)

Minnesota Valley Funeral Home, New Ulm, MN (507-354-2312/507-354-5446) ewarmka@comcast.net mvfh.com

Ohio Cleveland Memorial Society (216-751-5515) info@clevememorialsociety.org clevememorialsociety.org

Memorial Societies in Canada:

British Columbia Memorial Society of British Columbia, Vancouver, BC (604-733-7705/1-888-816-5902) mail@memorialsoc.org memorialsocietybc.org

Denman Island Memorial Society info@denmanisland.ca visitdenmanisland.ca

Alberta Cooperative Memorial Society, Calgary, AB (403-248-2044/1-800- 566-9959) calgarymemorial.com.admin@calgarymemorial.com

Saskatchewan Funeral Advisory and Memorial Society of Saskatchewan, Saskatoon, SK (306-374-5190) info@famss.ca famss.ca

Funeral Advisory and Memorial Society (FAMS), Kitchener, ON (416-461-6274) info@fams.ca www.fams.ca

L'Arche Canada Aging and Disability Services, Montreal, Quebec (514-844-1661) office@larche.ca

Funeral Co-operatives in Canada:

New Brunswick Fundy Funeral Home, Saint John, NB (506-646-2424)

Passage Funeral Co-operative, Shediac Bridge, NB (506-532-1050/1-888-532-1050) info@passagefc.ca

Passage Funeral Chapel, Moncton, NB (506-855-1145/1-888-532-1050) info2@passagefc.ca

Chartersville Funeral Home, Dieppe, NB (506-857-1901/1-888-532-1050) info2@passagefc.ca

Nova Scotia Sunset Funeral Co-operative, Margaree Valley, NS (902-248- 2991) sunsetfuneralco.op@gmail.com sunsetfuneralco-op.com

Arimathea Funeral Co-operative, Musquodoboit, NS (902-758-5034) arimatheafuneral.ca

Ontario Funeral Co-operative of Ottawa Inc. (613-288-2689) info@fco-cfo.coop fco-cfo.coop

The Cooperative Funeral Home of the District of Sudbury 705-566-2100 generalmail@cooperativefuneraire.ca cooperativefuneralhome.ca

The Funeral Cooperatives Network - La Fédération des coopératives funéraires du Québec (FCFQ): Sherbrooke, PQ Jimmy Fournier, Director of Human Resources. (819-566-6303 x 225) jfournier@fcfq.coop info@fcfq.coop www.fcfq.coop

Prince Edward Island Funeral Co-operatives of PEI www.peifuneralcoops.com

Sunrise Funeral Co-operative sunrisefuneral.coop

Death Care Advocacy Groups in the UK:

The Natural Death Centre, Winchester (01962 712 690) Est. 1991, a social, educational charity that gives free, impartial advice on all aspects of dying, bereavement and consumer rights.

Advocacy Focus (UK) (0300 323 0965) (Text: 07886 744 634) Email: advocacyfocus.org.uk

AGE UK Age UK Advice Line: (0800 678 1602) media@ageuk.org.uk

Humanist Ceremonies Humanists UK London EC1V 8BB (020 7324 3060) ceremonies@humanists.uk

Centre for Death and Society (University of Bath)

Death Care Advocacy Groups in Australia:

Natural Death Advocacy Network (ndan.com.au) is a growing Australian network and advocacy partnership of community facilitators, professionals, activists, and educators working to enrich the experience of dying and death.

Compassionate Communities Australia is part of a global movement of communities working to improve how we care for one another, especially during illness, death, and challenging times.

Grief Australia (+61 3 9265 2100) info@grief.org.au Education and Training Enquiry: education@grief.org.au Membership Enquiry: membership@grief.org.au

Holistic End of Life and Deathcare Australia. info@held.org.au HELD is an organization dedicated to promoting and providing holistic approaches to end-of-life care, death care practices, after-death care, and funeral care in Australia.

Palliative Care Australia (02 6232 0700). For information about palliative care services, see PCA's National Palliative Care Service Directory.

Natural Death Care Centre (+61 0427 924 310) naturaldeathcarecentre.org

Death Care Advocacy Groups in New Zealand:

Death Without Debt www.deathwithoutdebt.org.nz deathwithoutdebt@proton.me

Grief Centre New Zealand Counselling, support groups and general enquiries admin@griefcentre.org.nz (09 418 1457/0800 331 333)

Bpac.org.nz (Better medicine New Zealand) contact@bpac.org.nz editor@bpac.org.nz

Addendum 2: Bibliography

Books on the End of Life and Management of Grief:

The American Way of Death Revisited by Jessica Mitford *(First Vintage Books, Reprint ed. 1998).* "A funny and unforgiving book is the best memento mori we are likely to get." – New York Review of Books

"I don't know what to say" by Dr. Robert Buckman (First Vintage Books,1989). "A clear and intensely moving handbook in death, with not one punch pulled." – The Times (London)

Confessions of a Funeral Director: How Death Saved My Life by Caleb Wilde (Harper One, 2018).

All the Ways Our Dead Still Speak: A Funeral Director on Life, Death and the Hereafter by Caleb Wilde (Broadleaf Books, 2022).

The Profits of Death: An Insider Exposes the Death Care Industries by Darryl J. Roberts (Five Star Publications, 1997). "I can't think of a better person to blow the whistle in the funeral industry" – Lisa Carlson, former director of the Funeral Ethics Organization in the U.S..

Final Rights: Reclaiming the American Way of Death by Joshua Slocum and Lisa Carlson (Upper Access Inc., 2011).

Elderhood: Redefining Aging, Transforming Medicine, Reimagining Life by Louise Aronson (Bloomsbury

Publishing, Reprint ed. 2021).

Our Last Best Act: Planning for the End of Our Lives to Protect the Places and People We Love by Mallory McDuff (Broadleaf Books, 2021).

Is the Cemetery Dead? by David Charles Sloane (University of Chicago Press, 2018).

A Good Goodbye: Funeral Planning for Those Who Don't Plan to Die by Gail Rubin (Light Tree Press, 2010). "Talking about sex won't make you pregnant, and talking about funerals won't make you dead."

Being Peace by Tich Nhat Hanh (Parallax Press, 2005). "An exquisite meditation on being peace in order to make peace. A book for everyone concerned about the state of the world and the quality of our lives."

Death to Dust by Kenneth Iverson, MD. (Glen Press, 1994).

A Beginner's Guide to the End: Practical Advice for Living Life and Facing Death by Dr. B.J. Miller and Shoshana Berger (Simon and Schuster, 2020).

The Art of Dying Well: A Practical Guide to a Good End of Life by Katy Butler (Scribner, Reprint ed. 2019).

Grave Matters by Mark Harris (Scribner, Reprint ed. 2008).

Rest in Peace: Insider's Tips to the Low Cost, Low Stress Funeral by Brian Burkhardt (Morgan James Publishing, 2008).

The Green Burial Guidebook: Everything You Need to Plan an Affordable, Environmentally Friendly Funeral by Elizabeth Fournier (New World Library, 2018)

Greening Death: Reclaiming Burial Practices and Restoring Our Tie to the Earth by Suzanne Kelly. (Rowman & Littlefield Publishers, 2017).

When Death Speaks by Stephen Garrett (Friesen Press, 2013).

On Death and Dying: What the Dying Have to Teach Doctors, Nurses, Clergy and Their Own Families by Elisabeth Kübler-Ross (Scribner, Reissued 2014). The ground-breaking classic on the five stages of grief.

The Art of Dying by Peter and Elizabeth Fenwick (Continuum, 2008). Neuropsychiatrist Peter Fenwick believes consciousness may survive the death of the brain.

Click Here When I Die: Making Things Easier for Those You Love by Jonathan S. Braddock (Lioncrest, 2017)

Talking about Death Won't Kill You: The Essential Guide to End-of-Life Conversations by Dr. Kathy Kortes-Miller. (ECW Press, 2018).

The Good Funeral by Thomas Long and Thomas Lynch (Westminster John Knox Press, 2013).

Books for Those Under 20:

Finding the Words: How to talk to children and teens about death by Dr. Alan D. Wolfelt (Companion Press).

Straight Talk About Death for Teenagers by Earl A. Grollman (Beacon Press).

When Someone You Love Has Died by Stephanie Seidler (Cuddlebug Books, 2022).

I Can't Believe They're Gone: A kid's grief book by Karen Brough (self-published).

Feeling All My Grief by Kim T.S. (self-published).

We Need to Talk About Death by Sarah Chavez (Neon Squid, 2024).

What Happens When a Loved One Dies? by Dr. Jillian Roberts (Orca Books, 2022).

Websites:

Funeral Consumers Alliance:

https://funerals.org/consumers/

National Home Funeral Alliance: homefuneralalliance.org info@homefuneralsallance.org

Global Green Burial Alliance globalgreenburialalliance.net

People's Memorial Association:

https://peoplesmemorial.org

Green Burial Council (United States and Canada):

www.greenburialcouncil.org

Final Passages: https://finalpassages.org

Seven Ponds, El Cerrito (Albany), California: www.sevenponds.com

Home-funerals.html U.S. Funerals Online: https://www.us-funerals.com

The Funeral Rule (U.S. Federal Trade Commission): www.consumer.ftc.gov/articles/0300-ftc-funeral-rule

Confessions of a Funeral Director (Caleb Wilde blog): https://www.calebwilde.com

National Funeral Directors Association (U.S.): https://nfda.org

Funeral Association of Canada: https://www.fsac.ca

National Society of Allied and Independent Funeral Directors (UK): https://saif.org.uk 172

Afterword – The new standard in funeral management (U.S.): www.afterword.com

Funeral Help Center: www.funeralhelpcenter.com

Dying with Dignity: https://www.dyingwithdignity.ca/

In the Light Turns: https://inthelightturns.com

The Art of Dying Well, TED talk by Dr. Peter Fenwick: https:// www.youtube.com/watch?v=U-CXpReUpiM

End of Life Doula Association of Canada https:ß//endoflifedoulaassociation.org

Federation of Burial and Cremation Authorities: https://www.fbca.org.uk/

Home Funeral Directory: www.homefuneralalliance.org

Body Donation: donatelifeamerica@donatelife.net

Green Burial Society of Canada:
http://www.greenburialcanada.ca/

Funeral Advisory and Memorial Society:
https://www.fams.ca

Memorial Society of BC: https://memorialsocietybc.org/

Organ Donation:

www.giftoflife.on.ca/en/aboutus.htm

Federation des Cooperatives due Quebec
https://www.fcfq. coop/

Death Benefit:

https://www.canada.ca/en/services/benefits/publicpensio
ns/cpp/cppdeath-benefit.html

Addendum 3: Insightful Observations on Mortality

"Even death is not to be feared by one who has lived life wisely." – Siddhartaa Guutama (Buddha), (between the 6th and 4th centuries BCE)

"Our death is our wedding with eternity." – Rumi, 13th-century Islamic poet and mystic (1207-1273).

"If you don't know how to die, don't worry; Nature will tell you what to do on the spot, fully and adequately. She will do this job perfectly for you; don't bother your head about it." – Michel de Montaigne, 16th-century French philosopher (1533-1592).

"It seems to me most strange that men should fear, seeing that death, a necessary end, will come when it will come." – William Shakespeare (1564-1616).

"To live in hearts we leave behind is not to die." – Thomas Campbell, Scottish Poet (1777-1844)

"Our dead are never dead to us, until we have forgotten them." – George Eliot (1819-1880).

"The fear of death follows from the fear of life. A man who lives fully is prepared to die at any time." – Mark Twain (Samuel Langhorne Clemens), American writer, humorist (1835-1910).

"Death is not the end. There remains the litigation over the estate." – Ambrose Bierce, American writer, journalist, poet, and Civil War veteran (1842-1914).

"If you wish to be remembered, then leave a lot of debts." – Elbert Hubbard, American writer, artist, and philosopher. (1865-1914).

"It is very beautiful over there." – Thomas Edison, American inventor (1847-1931).

"One never knows the ending. One has to die to know what exactly happens after death, although Catholics have their hopes." – Alfred Hitchcock, filmmaker (1899-1980).

"Live as if you were to die tomorrow. Learn as if you were to live forever." – Mohandas (Mahatma) Gandhi. (1869-1948).

"Do not seek death. Death will find you. But seek the road that makes death a fulfillment." – Dag Hammarskjöld, UN Secretary-General (1953-1961)

"Old friends pass away, new friends appear. It is just like the days. An old day passes, a new day arrives. The important thing is to make it meaningful." – Tenzin Gyato, Dalai Lama. (1935-)

"I have lived with the prospect of an early death for the last forty-nine years. I'm not afraid of death, but I'm in no hurry to die. I regard the brain as a computer which will stop working when its components fail. There is no heaven or afterlife for broken down computers; that is a fairy story for people afraid of the dark." – Stephen Hawking (1942-2018)

"Death is death is not the opposite of life but a part of it." – Haruki Murakami, Japanese writer (1949-)

"Death is a destination we all share. No one has ever escaped it, and that is as it should be, because death is very likely the single invention of life. It clears out the old and makes way for the new." – Steve Jobs (1955-2011)

Acknowledgments

My special thanks to Linda Sutton, retired news editor of The Toronto Star, University of Western Ontario journalism, and my invaluable in-house copy editor, advisor, and dear friend for 58 years.

About the Author

Ian Sutton has been a journalist for more than 60 years. He has worked as a radio news director and a reporter at major Canadian newspapers, including The Toronto Star, as well as national magazines. He specialized in environmental, disability, aging, and healthcare issues. Born in Smiths Falls, Ontario, he now lives in a multi-generational household in Yarmouth, Nova Scotia.

Index

www.ingramcontent.com/pod-product-compliance
Lightning Source LLC
Chambersburg PA
CBHW071608210326
41597CB00019B/3453